Inside the Customer
Universe

Inside the Customer Universe

How to Build Unique Customer
Insight for Profitable Growth and
Market Leadership

Henrik Andersen & Thomas Ritter

John Wiley & Sons, Ltd

Other Wiley Editorial Offices

John Wiley & Sons Inc., 111 River Street, Hoboken, NJ 07030, USA

Jossey-Bass, 989 Market Street, San Francisco, CA 94103-1741, USA

Wiley-VCH Verlag GmbH, Boschstr. 12, D-69469 Weinheim, Germany

John Wiley & Sons Australia Ltd, 42 McDougall Street, Milton, Queensland 4064, Australia

John Wiley & Sons (Asia) Pte Ltd, 2 Clementi Loop #02-01, Jin Xing Distripark, Singapore
129809

John Wiley & Sons Canada Ltd, 6045 Freemont Blvd. Mississauga, Ontario, L5R 4J3 Canada

Wiley also publishes its books in a variety of electronic formats. Some content that appears in
print may not be available in electronic books.

Library of Congress Cataloging-in-Publication Data

Andersen, Henrik, 1953-
  Inside the customer universe: how to build unique customer insight for profitable growth
and market leadership / Henrik Andersen, Thomas Ritter.
    p. cm.
  Includes bibliographical references and index.
  ISBN 978-0-470-69424-4 (cloth : alk. paper)   1. Customer relations.   2. Marketing.
I. Ritter, Thomas, 1970- II. Title.
  HF5415.5.A525   2008
  658.8'343—dc22

                                                                                    2008015120

British Library Cataloguing in Publication Data

A catalogue record for this book is available from the British Library

ISBN 978-0-470-69424-4 (HB)

Typeset in 11/16pt Trump Medieval by SNP Best-set Typesetter Ltd., Hong Kong
Printed and bound in Great Britain by TJ International Ltd, Padstow, Cornwall, UK

Contents

Preface

Learning is often described as a voyage of discovery. Our voyage into the customer universe began in the fall of 2004. While talking about challenges in business life, we realized that we both were trying to solve similar problems: These problems were with customer segmentation. And as travel is often nicer with company, we embarked on a joint voyage.

Our original idea was to find a valid segmentation framework useful for firms – that was as precise as we were able to put it at the time. We had been down the road of statistically significant segmentation models realizing that no matter how many Greek letters we employed, implementing segmentation gave no significant impact on profit. Something was wrong – not with the models but with the customers who apparently behaved like moving targets showing little if any sign of consistency. In contrast, by looking at ourselves, our family members, and friends and colleagues, their behaviors seemed reasonably consistent to us and they did not seem to change. And thanks for that: If they constantly changed their behaviors in unpredictable ways how could we trust these people being close to us? Generally, people are not changing behaviors radically as implied by some segmentation models. If so there would be no social order, no collaboration, no friendships, no trust and no loyalty.

Many hours have since been spent in our offices, in meeting rooms, at conferences (scenes) discussing concepts, running workshops, implementing sales tools (roles) – oh yes, ever since we worked out that types, roles and scenes are the dimensions, we couldn't stop using them.

There was no tour plan for the voyage, nor did we make tour shirts of our voyage. In hindsight, the first leg was on customer types. Henrik had done some projects on identifying "real customers" and this soon became our dimension customer types. And then roles and scenes. It has taken us a few discussions to sort these dimensions out – we had the cases but we were missing the words. We finally had a segmentation framework that worked. Actually, after knowing the result, we cannot imagine that it seemed difficult at the start. That reminded us of the Egg of Columbus:

> The story about Columbus goes that after he had discovered America he attended a dinner which a Spanish gentleman gave in his honor. At the dinner a person began scoffing at the admiral's success in finding the new world, stating that what Columbus had been doing was the simplest thing in the world. Anybody can do it – just sail across the ocean and coast along the islands!

In reply, Columbus asked all the gentlemen in attendance to make an egg stand on end. After all the men tried and failed, they stated that it was impossible. Columbus then placed the egg's small end on the table, breaking the shell a bit, so that it could stand upright. Columbus then stated that it was "the simplest thing in the world. Anybody can do it, after he has been shown how!"

(adapted from Wikipedia)

For us, CUBEical segmentation is like the Egg of Columbus: It is easy once shown how. While preparing for landing from our voyage and writing the first book draft two years ago, we ended up with a problem. The conclusion chapter became longer and longer as all these things kept appearing which our segmentation model solved. So instead of disembarking and publishing a book on good segmentation, we refueled and continued our voyage. Despite having the customer universe map, we didn't have a map for this part either. We just went after the stars – but we found three maps which today are our version of developing a strategy.

From here, it was turbulent. We did implement solutions, saw how people in organizations started sharing knowledge without being pushed to do so. We were also allowed to fly through fast moving consumer goods universes and key account management universes to explore some challenging territory. Some jolly good trips.

Now we have landed. Maybe a bit overwhelmed by the trip's impressions. We hope that our travel guide transports the enthusiasm we have for the topic, the richness of ideas and data which is in that area, the appreciation of all those people we are indebted to. And we hope the business management framework CUBEical Thinking makes as much sense to you as it makes to us.

What did we learn on the voyage? Well, it is in this book. Enjoy it.

Henrik Andersen

Thomas Ritter

Copenhagen, January 2008

1

A quick guide to Customer Universe Based Execution

E VERY EXECUTIVE STRIVES HARD FOR BETTER EARNINGS before interest, tax, depreciation and amortization – EBITDA has become the language of executives. While focusing on building long-lasting profitable customer relationships based on true customer loyalty, most find themselves in a position where fulfilling this objective seems to be an uphill battle where one essential framework is missing – a model of the customer universe.

In this book we present our view on the customer universe and on how executives can base their execution on insights about the customer universe. Our main message is that profitable revenue growth can only be achieved by Customer Universe Based Execution, we call this CUBEical Thinking. CUBEical Thinking is a business management framework – a new way of thinking business. It is strongly rooted in understanding customers in their universe, so we apply a holistic view of customers with all the complexities of today's markets. We do not make the universe flat to achieve simplicity; rather, we try to describe the customer universe as complexly as necessary but in consistent terms thereby making the description simple and intuitively recognizable. CUBEical Thinking enables strategy development and implementation and does not stop at customer insight – so it is not "only" a marketing tool. It provides a common view and language about customers to firms – so it enables firm-wide implementation and avoids island solutions.

CUBEical Thinking – a business management framework

By introducing our concept of CUBEical Thinking, we will demonstrate how any firm can make sense of customers, create true customer loyalty, realize profitable revenue growth and potentially obtain market leadership. CUBEical Thinking is a business management framework building on three elements (Figure 1.1):

1. **CUBEical segmentation**, which provides a stable segmentation framework predicting customer needs and thereby providing firms with the platform for becoming market leaders by understanding and setting customers' expectations. Based on the three dimensions of customer types, roles and scenes, the competitive arenas of a firm are defined. These arenas or submarkets, where the interactions with customers take place and where the firm meets its competitors, are easy to understand for everybody and thus easy to communicate across the organization. The unique features of CUBEical segmentations are:

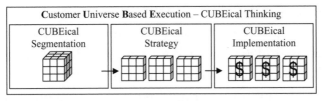

Figure 1.1   The CUBEical Thinking business management framework.

- The stability of the segmentation – overcoming unpredictable segment membership changes;

- The recognizable real life description of customers – overcoming the artificial average driven statistical segment descriptions;

- The handling of customer complexity through roles and scenes – overcoming the unrealistic one-segment-fits-all-occasions problem.

Herewith, CUBEical segmentation is breaking new ground in customer segmentation by overcoming the shortcomings of current segmentation practices that block the road for customers to become the pivotal focus for the executive agenda of driving profitable revenue growth.

2. **CUBEical strategy**, which builds on CUBEical segmentation and provides a firm with a roadmap of where and how to compete. Identifying competitive arenas, which are important to customers, possible to access for the firm, and profitable to serve, is the key foundation of a sound business strategy to achieve true customer loyalty. CUBEical strategy provides the framework for generating

true loyalty by securing that all three areas of the customer and supplier universe are aligned: (1) mutual value is created (delivery for both parties); (2) customer needs and expectations match the firm's competencies and offerings (promise for mid-term developments); and (3) customer and supplier types fit, roles are aligned and scenes matched (foundation match for long-term development). The unique features of CUBEical strategy are:

- A truly customer-driven strategy foundation – not just lip-service, but insight based;

- A strategy defined towards detailed competitive arenas, not markets – by understanding markets as combinations of competitive arenas, resource allocation becomes more precise and action oriented – instead of pointing out a target market and leaving the inner market mechanics as a black box.

Herewith, CUBEical strategy is breaking new ground in strategy development as it is directly rooted in the customer universe through the CUBEical segmentation framework. It integrates all functional substrategies into one strategy for where and how to compete within a market in general and the individual customer universe in particular.

3. **CUBEical implementation** is our way of implementing the strategy through tailored and highly targeted marketing (i.e. targeted communication), sales (i.e. realizing cross- and up-sales potential) and new product develop-

ment initiatives (i.e. focused innovation efforts). The unique features of CUBEical implementation are:

- One common language, from top management to shop floor level, from sales and marketing to accounting, from business people to engineers;

- One face to the customer – because everybody knows the customers;

- Targeted sales and marketing efforts to increase sales and marketing effectiveness;

- Targeted customer relationship management (CRM) system to support sales and marketing in realizing cross- and up-sales potential.

CUBEical implementation improves strategy implementation by providing a platform for learning from customers and markets. CUBEical implementation enables harvesting, structuring and sharing customer and market knowledge. It leads the way to effective marketing and sales programs where resources are invested with great impact on customers. Impact is measurable and CUBEical implementation can be documented at the top and bottom line as profitable revenue growth.

CUBEical Thinking reveals customers' needs and enables firms to proactively set customers' expectations beyond the reach of the competition. The strange marketing claim that firms have to surprise their customers by exceeding expectations in order to be successful is not only outdated, but conceptually wrong. Exceeding customer expectations every time is simply impossible – at least for a profit. Furthermore, surprised customers have not paid for the feature they are so happy with, so revenue potential has not been utilized.

The dimensions and elements of the customer universe

Managers need to think beyond expectations and uncover the drivers of expectations. But this is easier said than done. Expectations are, of course, driven by customer needs. But there seems to exist some general agreement that customer needs are inaccessible with respect to market research and that the drivers of customer needs are unknown – at least they have been until now. Through our research, we have decoded the foundation of the customer universe and thereby identified the drivers of customer needs: customer type, roles and scenes. These three dimensions define the customer universe and are the building blocks of CUBEical segmentation.

But let's start in the well-known sector of the customer universe (Figure 1.2). Being unable to pin down the needs of customers, firms try to reveal the extent to which customers feel that the firm fulfills their needs. In order to gain an overview of the situation, these firms spend millions of dollars on customer satisfaction reviews and on segmenting their customer base accordingly into ambassadors, neutral customers, or "terrorists". But still, even the highly satisfied ambassadors

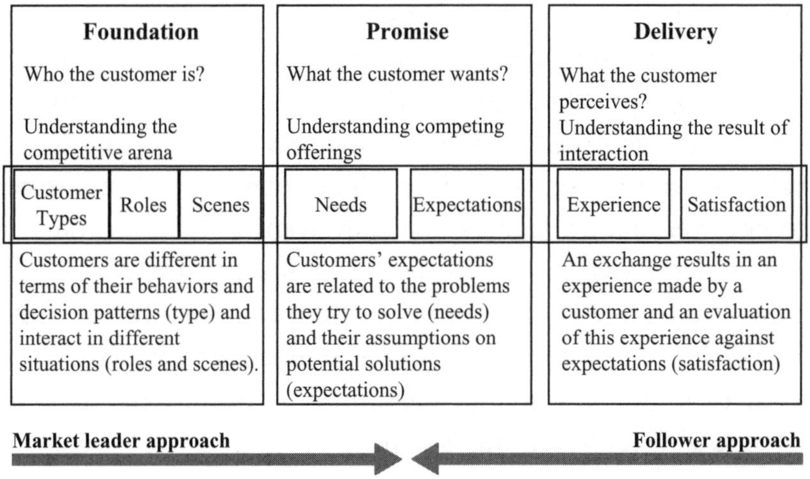

Foundation			Promise			Delivery		
Who the customer is? Understanding the competitive arena			What the customer wants? Understanding competing offerings			What the customer perceives? Understanding the result of interaction		
Customer Types	Roles	Scenes	Needs		Expectations	Experience		Satisfaction
Customers are different in terms of their behaviors and decision patterns (type) and interact in different situations (roles and scenes).			Customers' expectations are related to the problems they try to solve (needs) and their assumptions on potential solutions (expectations)			An exchange results in an experience made by a customer and an evaluation of this experience against expectations (satisfaction)		

Market leader approach ▶ ◀ Follower approach

Figure 1.2 Dimensions and elements of the customer universe.

are churning. Executives start realizing that satisfaction scores are not only weak loyalty predictors but that satisfaction studies offer little, if any, insights into possible improvements. Goods and service improvements cannot be derived from satisfaction reviews because the causes of dissatisfaction are not revealed sufficiently.

In order to overcome the blindness of customer satisfaction reviews, progressive firms engage in customer experience studies. When a customer signals dissatisfaction, the natural question is: What did you experience with our firm that made you dissatisfied? By mapping customer activity cycles, insights are gained into the experiences made on a customer's trip through the cycle. Therewith, improvements can be made to give customers a better experience – within the cycle. Insights regarding radical innovations are hard to find that way around.

Digging deeper into the customer universe, firms start to analyze customer expectations, i.e. what customers want to experience throughout their activity cycle. This type of analysis opens executives' minds towards new thoughts and innovations. But one fundamental problem remains: If firms want to become market leaders, i.e. they want to set an industry agenda and move customers' expectations, executives need to explore customers' expectations before customers tell them. Marketing has to do with expectation management – so firms need to know and predict customers' expectations. This is what CUBEical Thinking is about.

One striking characteristic of satisfaction, experience and expectation is their dynamic nature. Customers' expectations, their experiences and their satisfaction scores change frequently. Insurance companies and banks are now expected to send personalized letters, aircrafts feature internet connections and food is supposed to be ecologically produced. With technological development progressing, expectations are moving targets. Likewise, experiences depend on many things along the customer activity cycle. Every experience is new by definition, and thus satisfaction is subject to change. Satisfied customers become dissatisfied, and vice versa. Consequently, expectation, experience and satisfaction seem to be moving targets and thereby doubtful as a bearing point for strategy and execution. To base corporate strategies or innovation programs on such measures is a dangerous undertaking.

The concept of customer loyalty implies that long-term relationships are founded on shared values and beliefs vis-à-vis the firm and its customers, not just on satisfactory fulfillment of promises (Figure 1.2). Taking this approach to loyalty, CUBEical Thinking explains the stable foundation for building long-lasting relationships based on aligning the customer universe with the supplier universe. True customer loyalty is the result of setting customer expectations beyond the reach of competition and is based on insights into the customers' universe. Customers are not moving targets, as many believe them to be. Dynamics exist within the stable competitive arenas of the customer universe.

Discovering the customer universe

The first part of the book invites the reader to discover the customer universe. In Chapter 2, we discuss the executive challenge of driving EBITDA growth and how customers fit into this challenge. The lack of customer focus in boardrooms is a result of a translation problem between the customer-facing departments (e.g. sales, marketing, service) and the C level (e.g. CEO, executives, management). In order to solve this, we define three executive requirements and translate them into criteria for good segmentation. Only by meeting the criteria for good segmentation can customers become the pivotal focus on the executive agenda.

In Chapter 3, we discuss current segmentation practices in relation to the criteria of good segmentation. We follow up on this discussion by introducing customer types in Chapter 4 and roles and scenes in Chapter 5. These three aforementioned elements provide firms with a deep insight into their customers' needs. We combine these three dimensions and outline our CUBEical segmentation approach in Chapter 6.

Customer types

The values and beliefs of an individual person or an organization are generally assumed to be mirrored in the behavior and the decisions of the person or organization in question. Thus, it is widely accepted that people and organizations differ; for example, in terms of their risk orientation (some like uncertainty, others prefer predictability), their orientation towards others (extrovert vs introvert), their orientation to nature and sustainability, etc. Values and beliefs drive people's and organizations' overall behaviors either consciously or unconsciously and define their type. In Chapter 4, we explain how firms can identify customer types and why such segmentation lives up to the executive requirements of good segmentation.

Roles

Many firms regard a customer as one customer. That is in most cases a fatal mistake. Having this one-face-fits-all attitude mistreats customers and is often a sign of not being customer oriented. Customers are multi-individuals, i.e. they perform different roles in their interaction with a supplier. Like an actress, customers have, or play, different roles. Therefore, we use the role concept to capture these differences.

Roles are defined in relation to other people – or firms in case of business markets. Typical roles are egoist (only thinking of oneself, i.e. being alone), mother-father-sister-brother (in relation to family), employee (in relation to a boss), colleague (in relation to co-workers) and functional position (in relation to customers and suppliers). We are very used to shifting roles, often many times a day. Sometimes, we are even performing different roles simultaneously such as when taking a mobile phonecall (business) while minding the kids (father/mother).

Airlines, railway operators and car rental agencies often express blindness to customer roles. These firms have customer loyalty cards and claim they know their customers, but they never know in which role the customer is in when standing in front of them. The busy executive is not interested in a stay-over deal when the plane is overbooked, but the romantic partner on a weekend getaway may consider it. A simple question about the purpose of the trip at the desk would not only be friendly, but could make a big difference in the level of customer understanding and interaction.

The focus on roles solves some major problems conventional segmentation approaches have. First, it allows treating a customer according to his current, actual role and not to some average expected behavior of that customer. Understanding customers as "multividuals" goes one step further towards true customer orientation, i.e. understanding customers in their complexity and situational environment. We explore roles in Chapter 5.

By now we have a character (customer type) with a script (role), but we still need a scene to play to complete our CUBE-ical segmentation approach and thereby picture where and how interactions with customers take place and where and how competition unfolds.

Scenes

A firm meets a customer in different scenes. Scenes are physical objects, the resources which a customer has at hand. It makes a major difference if a person sits in a car, a train, on a bicycle or is walking. By varying the resources, i.e. the scene, different needs occur.

Scenes are the places and spaces of interaction – the environments. Customers move through different scenes: People drink Coke at home, on the go, in the office, or in a restaurant. Again, different needs are connected to different scenes, e.g. the two-liter bottle is more suitable for home drinking than on the go. Consider another scene shift, i.e. change in resources: The kind of beverage wanted changes with different meals, e.g. a hotdog, a salmon sandwich, roast beef, or a cake. Some will suggest other terms like occasion and situation to capture resource variation but these terms confuse more as they collapse customer type, roles and scenes. Our experience shows that executives can easily understand scenes in parallel with a theater – and they fully understand the business implications of finally being able to set the scene. Scenes are further discussed in Chapter 5.

Competitive arenas

Bringing the three elements, customer types, roles and scenes, together, we get our CUBEical segmentation framework (Figure 1.3). We call the subcubes "competitive arenas" because it is here competition unfolds. Customers with similar

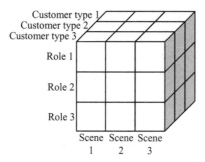

Figure 1.3 CUBEical segmentation framework.

needs search for solutions and firms compete to serve these customers. Firms that do not address the needs of a competitive arena are not competing because customers do not recognize them as interesting – these suppliers are simply not in the customers' universes.

In the CUBEical segmentation framework we capture the dynamics of customers in role and scene changes without having to change the segmentation model. This is a major advantage and differentiates CUBEical segmentation from other segmentation frameworks, which have problems in capturing and explaining customer complexity. Our approach offers a stable, intuitively understandable and easy-to-implement segmentation which is extremely powerful for strategy development and implementation.

Looking at the example of the cube shown in Figure 1.3, with its 27 distinct subcubes, or competitive arenas, many executives will at the first glance judge such a model as being perhaps too complex. However, the beauty of CUBEical segmentation is that it does not represent an artificially constructed framework but a structure within which all elements in all three dimensions – customer types, roles and scenes – are intuitively understandable and recognizable. Furthermore, it is not 27 segments that have to be memorized. In this case the segments are represented by the three customer types together with the few selected combinations of three roles and three scenes. Thus, customers are easily segmented, and the framework is easily adopted by firms and implemented across units, divisions and functions.

Activating the customer universe

In the second part of the book, we use the insights gained from the discovery of the customer universe to develop a strategy. CUBEical segmentation lays the foundation for CUBEical strategy, our concept for understanding and building true customer loyalty as further explained in Chapter 7. After having gained an understanding of the drivers of customer needs by performing CUBEical segmentation, executives must map the universe of their firm against their customers' universes. Firms also have values and beliefs (firm type), play their roles, and act in different scenes. But not all firms need to play all roles or in all scenes (e.g. some may not be present in all countries). A firm must have competencies that match the needs of the customer. These competencies enable the firm to create offerings that set customers' expectations. The offerings will be implemented (delivered, sent) leaving the customer with a satisfactory or unsatisfactory experience, and the firm with fulfillment and performance realization (see Figure 1.4).

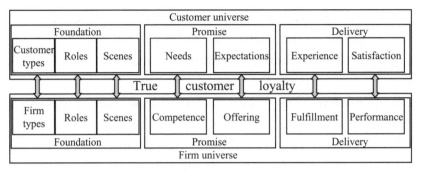

Figure 1.4 Aligning the customer and firm universe for true customer loyalty.

The CUBEical strategy framework has true customer orientation along the total customer universe at its core. True customer loyalty – commonly stated as the strategic target of firms – can only be achieved when a firm and a customer are aligned along the whole universe. A customer's initial experience must be positive and followed by a high degree of satisfaction; additionally, the firm must realize a positive delivery experience and satisfactory performance. Only when both sides create value for themselves will they be interested in conducting further business.

However, the firm–customer relationship develops over time. As such, both sides need to offer each other long-term perspectives which are based both on the firm's competencies and resulting offerings as well as on the customer's needs and expectations. This fit secures, at a minimum, a mid-term relationship as the basis is not only here and now but also tomorrow and the day after that.

Finally, true long-term relationships can only exist when firms and customers share their values and beliefs, play all necessary roles for each other, and meet in the scenes they enjoy playing in. True customer loyalty is achieved by capturing customers in their complexity and totality.

No firm has the resources to address all competitive arenas as identified through CUBEical segmentation. Thus, CUBEical strategy – in addition to addressing true customer loyalty – also provides the platform for making well-informed, transparent decisions of where and how to allocate and further develop the scarce resources of the firm.

Understanding the interplay between customers' segments and resources, firms realize that some customers are too far away to be reached, some are too insignificant to be interesting, and others are the black hole of losses. It is obvious that other suppliers' universes may be differently positioned – closer or further away from customers. It is in laying this strategic puzzle that firms decide which competitive arenas to compete within.

Once the overall strategy of the firm and the customer strategies have been defined through applying the CUBEical strategy framework, marketing and sales can develop their plans in order to gain a customer, to make the deal and utilize cross- and up-sales potential. We focus on CUBEical implementation in Chapter 8.

Marketing and sales plans take their departure in customer types and, through addressing the specific roles and scenes, firms can turn the gained insights into business action. CUBEical implementation in marketing is realized through better targeting of corporate branding, product branding and customer communications, while CUBEical implementation in sales is realized by leveraging customer relationships for up- and cross-selling. Through understanding customer needs by determining customer types, roles and scenes, firms can actively work with customers, efficiently brand themselves and sell the relevant part of their product portfolio.

Living the customer universe

The final part of the book deals with living the customer universe in day-to-day operations. In Chapter 9, we combine the different elements of segmentation, strategy and implementation into CUBEical Thinking, our business management framework. We explore CUBEical Thinking from a knowledge management perspective and discuss how CUBEical Thinking improves inner-firm communication on a day-to-day basis. One of the main headaches in business is lost customer knowledge – the lack of a consistent structure to accumulate customer intelligence. Not speaking the same language and not sharing vital customer information is the best way to waste resources. It is of paramount importance for firms to collect, distribute and act on customer knowledge. While this claim is not new, our frameworks offer the tools to achieve higher levels of customer knowledge management and avoid typical traps. Therewith, CUBEical Thinking provides a framework for integrating and consolidating all customer-facing activities in one transparent plan, across all functional areas within the firm.

We also dive into typical settings in business, the fast moving consumer goods universe (FMCG, Chapter 10) and the key account management universe (KAM, Chapter 11). In addition, we address the management of mergers and acquisitions – a major challenge for firms in their growth efforts (Chapter 12). We explain how CUBEical Thinking helps firms to live the customer universe in a consistent and effective manner. Our frameworks help reduce the inherent complexity – not by discarding complexity but by structuring complexity and, thus, making the customer universe manageable.

Summing up

Many executives are obsessed about customer retention: "Are my customers loyal?" This is, of course, extremely important. But true loyalty is more complex than satisfaction – true loyalty is built along the whole customer universe. By measuring and managing the end of the customer universe, i.e. satisfaction, executives are truly myopic and miss the opportunity to develop a sound foundation for customer loyalty. True loyalty is built on joint values and beliefs, matching roles and setting the scene – and by turning this into communicating and selling which is relevant for customers. Understanding this logic transfers business from reactive followers into loyalty leaders who set expectations.

Success depends on Customer Universe Based Execution – if executives understand customers in their universe, competitive advantage can be gained. This is the CUBEical logic. Firms can become market leaders by setting the rules of the game to the benefit of both their customers and themselves. As pointed out, customer types, roles and scenes are predictable and, therewith, behavior is predictable and stable. Since

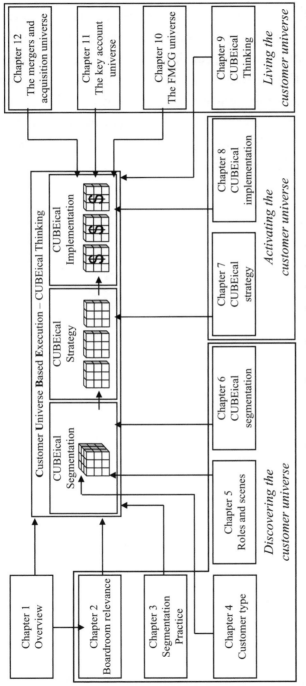

Figure 1.5 The roadmap for this book.

loyalty is about developing long-term, stable relationships based on mutual respect and value creation, CUBEical Thinking provides the appropriate frameworks and this book explains the different elements (Figure 1.5). Building and nursing customer relationships for mutual value creation are what lies at the core of CUBEical Thinking, and thereby at the core of CUBEical segmentation, CUBEical strategy and CUBEical implementation.

PART I

Discovering the customer universe

To start a discovery is never easy – where should one start? We found it natural to focus first on the internal decision-maker who allocates resources and demands results – the executives of firms. We are convinced that most of them are very aware of the importance of customers. But why is it that customer issues seldom make it to the top of the organization and to the top of the executive agenda? We explore the reasons for this in Chapter 2 and define the three executive requirements which any item tabled for the board meeting must meet to gain relevance. We also translate these requirements into good segmentation criteria.

In Chapter 3, we review common segmentation approaches and discuss their fit to the criteria of good segmentation. We notice some interesting concepts which we further develop in the subsequent chapters. We explain our notion of customer types in Chapter 4 and the issues around roles and scenes in Chapter 5. These three dimensions define the customer universe. To round up our discovery of the customer universe, we combine the three dimensions in Chapter 6.

2

The executive challenge of driving EBITDA growth

(Re-)Introducing customers to the executive agenda

The success of a firm's strategy is mirrored in its EBITDA growth – the performance yardstick of today's firms. It is on everybody's mind and all decision-makers know that low EBITDA results make the firm unattractive for shareholders, customers, employees and suppliers – all stakeholders react to weak financial performance. Successful executives have, therefore, a strong sense of what it takes to drive the profitability of their business. In addition, executives have a strong preference for growth. We have yet to meet the CEO who does not want their business to grow. Even though executives know that only growth in profits matters ("bottom-line growth"), many decisions are aimed at revenue growth ("top-line growth") – sometimes achieved at the expense of lower profits. The magic words for executives

Revenue	100	*CRM strategy*
Variable costs	–60	*Loyalty programs*
Contribution margin 1	40	Lean
Distribution costs	–10	Business process re-engineering
Contribution margin 2	30	Activity-based costing
Fixed costs		Outsourcing
		Off-shoring
• Administration, etc.	–5	CRM software
• Sales and marketing	–10	Sales automation
Profit (EBITDA)	15	*Sales training*

Figure 2.1 EBITDA equation and EBITDA growth initiatives (*market initiatives in italics*).

are profitable revenue growth – growing top-line and bottom-line simultaneously.

Successful executives know that the EBITDA equation (Figure 2.1) centers around a firm's output from both a resource perspective and a market perspective (Figure 2.2). This follows a return-on-investment logic: Firms "invest" resources into their processes (production, sales, marketing, R&D, management) which appear in the EBITDA equation as costs. The return on these investments are revenues which are determined by the volume sold and the prices charged. Thus, revenue depends on having offerings that customers value and on the ability to persuade customers to purchase them. This translates into two ways of driving EBITDA growth:

1. Growing resource efficiency: Resource efficiency is determined by the allocation of resources to an activity to achieve an output. Optimization of resource allocation is achieved either by producing as much of a given output as possible with given resources, or by reducing resources as much as possible while producing the same output. This relates to the internal efficiency of the firm. Over the

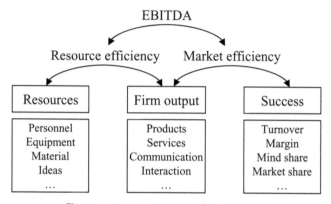

Figure 2.2 EBITDA growth elements.

past decades, executives have been busy with driving lean initiatives for minimizing variable production costs and time; initiating business process re-engineering (BPR) for optimizing work flow processes; shrinking the business scope to core competencies and off-shoring, or outsourcing remaining parts for achieving business excellence; implementing resource enterprise planning tools and software as well as activity-based costing for controlling resource allocation and increasing cost control – to mention a few of the many management concepts applied. Thus, this source of internally based EBITDA growth has been, and still is, in extreme focus.

While most departments of a firm have implemented these initiatives, the sales and marketing department has not really been affected. There have been experiments with lean selling – but the lean logic does not really translate into the sales area. While there have been huge projects of customer relationship management (CRM) and sales force automation (SFA), these initiatives have rarely shown the euphoric results for which they were sold. The old saying still holds true: "Half of all sales and marketing costs are spent without effect – but we do not know which half." In contrast, such a statement for purchasing and production is no longer thinkable.

While the resource efficiency of sales and marketing hereby still lag behind other departments, let's turn to the natural field of sales and marketing; the impact on customers and markets.

2. Growing market efficiency: Market efficiency is determined by a firm's market impact, i.e. a firm's ability to drive revenue through its competitive actions. As revenue is determined by sales volume and price, market efficiency depends on goods and services with excellent value propositions and targeted sales and marketing efforts. Thus, market efficiency depends heavily on customer insight and the implementation of these insights into product development and sales/marketing execution. Market efficiency growth is achieved by making the firm's output more valuable for customers so that they will buy more and pay higher prices.

Unfortunately, not many concepts to increase market efficiency have hit the corporate boardrooms. The CRM and lean projects within sales and marketing have generally not been successful. At best, they resulted in increased resource efficiency but unintentionally and unfortunately at the expense of decreasing market efficiency. The market orientation wave, the CRM wave and one-to-one relationship wave challenged the general philosophy of executives but did not offer any manageable revenue growth initiatives. User-driven and outcome-driven innovation, price optimization and value model building are seen as too operational for being relevant to the executive board.

As Figure 2.3 indicates, most industries have implemented their resource efficiency programs and, thus, have a high industry average as compared to market efficiency. Plotting a firm and its competitors into the efficiency map, we have indicated typical positions.

Our research shows that the curves of equal EBITDA results are often close to a rectangle shape: In competitive markets, EBITDA is rather "trade-off sensitive" – a small decrease in market efficiency requires significant improvement in resource efficiency (or vice versa) to achieve the same EBITDA result.

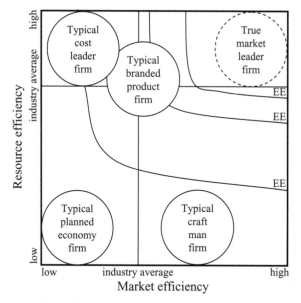

Figure 2.3 Efficiency map (EE = equal EBITDA curve).

This effect explains why standardization and modularization initiatives often have negative results beyond the initial investment costs. Most executives justify disappointing results in the first two years with increased (unexpected) implementation costs and later with market changes. In all too many cases, resource efficiency programs (lean, BPR, etc.) have resulted in lower market efficiency with detrimental EBITDA results. The exact shape of an equal-EBIDTA (EE) curve is industry specific depending on customer readiness to change suppliers when prices or features change.

Most firms face a situation where their resource efficiency is comparably high simply because the management concepts developed and implemented during the last decades primarily support firms in driving resource efficiency. Thus, firms have unintentionally been pursuing EBITDA growth through cutting costs, streamlining business processes, and through employing one or more of the internally focused powerful concepts hidden behind the long row of abbreviations and buzz-words: BPR, JIT, lean, outsourcing, Six Sigma, ERP, CRM. As a consequence of these implementations, the industry average of resource efficiency is high and additional gains are now extremely costly. Therefore, the most feasible way to grow EBITDA at present is by increasing the firm's market efficiency.

Welcome to customers on the executive agenda!

With CUBEical Thinking, we will demonstrate how it is feasible to make customers the pivotal focus on the executive agenda for driving profitable revenue growth. We will show the way towards optimizing market efficiency and to market leadership strategies. Many opportunities exist as the frameworks to activate them have been missing up until now. Far too often, marketing resources are spent with minimal impact (Figure 2.4). Therefore, better marketing and sales effectiveness is not a matter of more resources, but a matter of better utilization of resources.

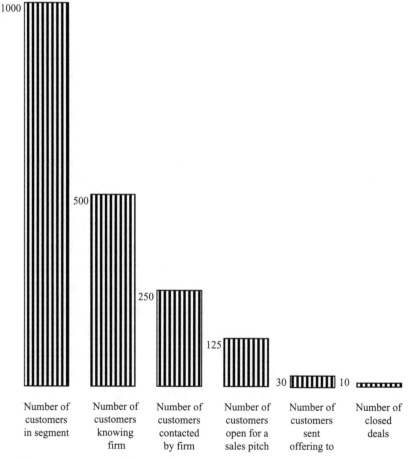

Figure 2.4 Typical number deflation between segment size and closed deals.

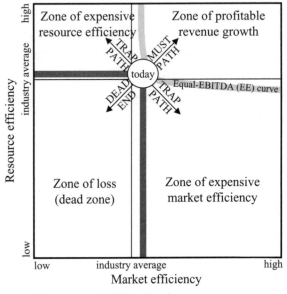

Figure 2.5 EBITDA development zones.

Figure 2.5 illustrates the EBITDA development zones for a given firm that is pursuing market leadership. Of course, there is only one valid zone for executives to consider – the one of higher EBITDA, indicated as "zone of profitable revenue growth". Often, initiatives get caught in traps: Resources may be minimized in a way such that the minimization becomes the focus of attention and happiness, rather than EBITDA growth. Alternatively, excited customers with high satisfaction scores are blinding the executives' view on the implied costs and, thus, EBIDTA implications. We consider these two zones as expensive because the cost of the efficiency increase outnumbers the returns on the bottom line.

Customers, of course, have had full executive attention during the recent decades due to the shift from the post-war marketplace – characterized by lack of goods and services – to today's market situation, characterized by abundant supply of goods and services. For achieving better EBITDA results, executives therefore know that their vision and strategy must:

- Specify which customers to target;

- Describe how to attract these customers and how to build long-term customer relationships and customer loyalty;

- Specify which competences to develop in order to serve the selected customers according to their needs and expectations.

Interestingly, executives have always known these three points. Even so, most attention has still been devoted to ad hoc initiatives aimed at offsetting the negative influence from the increased price pressure caused by the shift from the postwar shortage in goods and services to today's shortage in customers. Thus, even though executives talk about and surely have customer focus high on their agenda, this is not mirrored in the way EBITDA growth has been pursued. Consequently, the mantra of today's firms still seems to be:

By focusing on increasing productivity in production and logistics and by optimizing procurement and administration, we will do our best to offset the negative impact of the price pressure in the market threatening our EBITDA results. Herewith, we hope to maintain our current EBITDA level.

Of course, operational excellence and resource efficiency are a necessity. Firms should always strive to make continuous improvements in production and logistics, procurement and administration. However, for firms to stay competitive in today's market environments, customer focus and profitable top-line growth must have top priority on the executives' agenda alongside the optimization of cost structures.

But why is this so difficult? Simply because executives and customer-facing employees have been lacking proper tools for transforming the firm's tacit customer knowledge into explicit customer knowledge that can be structured, shared and leveraged upon when developing and implementing market leader strategies.

Customer knowledge is structured in the firm's customer segmentation framework and, due to inadequate segmentation practices, executives have been blindfolded regarding customer insights. Still they say:

If only we knew what's on the minds of our customers.

By demonstrating how it is feasible to make customers the pivotal focus on the executive agenda of driving profitable revenue growth, we will untie the Gordian knot of segmentation which has hindered sales and marketing from properly introducing customers to the executive agenda.

Executive requirements for customer insights

Our research reveals that the paradox of customers being both at the forefront of the executives' minds and on the outskirts of the executive agenda can be traced back to inadequate segmentation practice and thereby to the translation problem between the boardroom and the customer-facing departments. Currently, executives do not get the required input for their decision-making according to three fundamental executive requirements:

1. *Context*: Executives require the presentation of business issues in a clear context. A 30-page statistical description of average customers in different groups does not fit the requirements. Like the famous one-minute-elevator-speech, issues must be presented in a context where the executives can easily and quickly recognize the important elements to focus on. Thus, current customer segmentation has not provided a clear context for discussing customer issues.

2. *Accountability*: Executives are held accountable for driving the long-term development of the firm through creating visions, developing strategies to achieve them, and securing a solid financial base to finance the strategy and to satisfy stakeholders. If issues change all the time for reasons that cannot be explained or predicted, executive decisions cannot be made and accountability becomes an illusion. Current segmentation practices with constantly changing customer needs and unpredictable market and technology dynamics do not meet executives' requirement for accountability in decision making.

3. *Result*: Executives are present in firms to deliver results. They are aware of the short- and long-term impact of their decisions. They want to move things and see things moving

– if not the full effect then at least a development process must be traceable. Executives are not interested in investments which *might* have an impact on profits, which potentially *could* be a good idea, or which *may* prove their true value in the future. If the impact of a decision cannot be predicted, the decision is likely not to be taken. This does not mean that executives do not think in different scenarios and do not accept some risk; but distinct concrete scenarios and calculated risks are desired. As the famous saying states: What you can't measure, you cannot manage. This translates in the executive boardroom to: I will not lead an execution if I cannot see a result. Current segmentation practices do not support strategic decisions as segmentation is hardly related to results.

Thus, sales and marketing do currently not fit the executives' requirements of context, accountability and results due to the lack of a proper segmentation practice. Instead of translating the sales and marketing world into the executive world in a common language, marketing and sales directors and managers are busy explaining to their executive boards why the customer differences which everybody knows exist are hard to recognize in the segmentation models, why customer behavior is unpredictable in contrast to real-life perceptions of stability and why marketing impact is difficult to trace. No wonder executives are sometimes concerned as to whether their marketing and sales departments have a firm grip on business – are things really unstable or are they accidentally made unstable?

Due to the inadequate customer segmentation, sales and marketing managers are caught in three challenges which thereby unintentionally prevent them from delivering the material required to facilitate the boardroom decisions.

Challenge One – How to capture differences between customers

Executives, as well as the customer-facing employees of the firm, know that their customers differ with regard to behaviors and their ways of making decisions. They can recognize the differences when they are in contact with customers. Consequently, it is of concern to executives when marketing and sales cannot make these differences recognizable in their segmentation models. Thus, current segmentation practices deliver materials which describe customers in terms of general variables that are unrelated to the experienced differences. But how can sales and marketing provide a recognizable picture of customers and thereby put customers into a context which makes business sense?

Challenge Two – How to capture the complexity of customers

Executives and customer-facing employees know that a customer lives in a dynamic world and often has many faces when in contact with a firm. They can recognize behavioral patterns of the same customer across a complex set of different situations. They know they must understand their customers in their totality, as well as the complex market structures in which customer interaction takes place. Consequently, executives and sales and marketing have their concerns about accountability when current segmentation practice places one customer in several segments at the same time and over time. Are customers really moving targets? By using customer segmentation, can sales and marketing really capture and link this diversity of situations in the marketplace to customers in a stable and structured manner which supports the requirements of accountability in decision-making?

Challenge Three – How to drive sales and marketing effectively

Executives and customer-facing employees know that achieving market results requires more than steering through the rear-view mirror. They know that market leadership requires foresight and insight into customers. But how can sales and marketing deliver a segmentation framework for deciding on the right road to market leadership? How can sales and marketing deliver and document results?

Executives are waiting for answers in terms of context, accountability and results. Sales and marketing managers are working hard on these challenges. Sorting them out will place customers on the executive agenda and wipe out the executive paradox of customers being both at the forefront of the executives' minds and on the outskirts of the executive agenda – as well as solving sales and marketing's problems in explaining their worth to the firm.

Let's look at the three challenges.

Addressing Challenge One – How to capture differences between customers

As pointed out above, most executives and customer-facing employees notice differences between customers. Thus, firms can segment their customers into groups of customers behaving similarly within a group and differently across groups. However, much segmentation operates with segment descriptions far away from "real" customers. As one manager said: "Our segments look good on paper and in the marketing department they even are logical. But standing outside the customers' headquarters five minutes before the meeting, no one can put the customer into one of these segments."

To be operational and, thus, of business value, segmentation must mirror the executive requirements of context, accountability and result – and not only for the benefit of the executive agenda:

- *Customer segments must be intuitively recognizable.* If not, the executives and customer-facing employees cannot differentiate between customers and a business strategy based on differentiation among customers will fail in its development and in its implementation. Segmentation must capture the real context of a customer in order to be understandable and manageable.

- *Customer segments must be stable with regard to segment membership.* If not, customers will be in one segment at one time and in another segment at another time. Which differentiation strategy should then apply?

Furthermore, if segment membership is not stable, segmentation cannot support knowledge sharing and leveraging the organization's joint customer knowledge.

- *Customer segments must be effective in the market by reflecting the needs and expectations of the customers.* If not, actions taken by the firm based on the segmentation make no sense to customers and thus implementation of the firm's strategy has no impact on revenues.

The three requirements are direct translations of the executive requirements – we consider the three as criteria for good segmentation practice. Our research shows that current segmentation practices fail to deliver on one or more of these three characteristics. Consequently, it has not been feasible in the past to make customers the pivotal focus on the executive agenda for optimizing a firm's EBITDA.

Addressing Challenge Two – How to capture the complexity of customers

A few years back in time, it was an acceptable attitude to describe customers as nomads between segments, unpredictably moving around in the marketplace. In the meantime, many firms have realized that their customers are not chaotic, nor are they unpredictable. The explanation of customer dynamics is found in the changing situation of the customer, not the change in the customer itself. This insight calls for the following understanding of markets:

A **market** is a set of social arrangements that allows buyers and sellers to discover information and carry out a voluntary exchange of goods or services.

Following this definition of a market, each situation in which a firm meets a customer represents a submarket – a social arrangement which is a part of the overall market. It is on these submarkets that the firm meets its competitors while competing for the hearts and wallets of customers. Therefore, we denote these submarkets as *competitive arenas*.

The increasing insight into these competitive arenas has led to a strong move towards situational consumption studies. Unfortunately, this move has not generated a stable base for executives' decision-making. On the contrary, executives are presented with long lists of seemingly random situations. Current segmentation practices do not support the above concept of competitive arenas. Therefore, these segmentation practices are not suited for mirroring actual customer behavior and for capturing the diversity of the marketplace in a way which can support context, accountability and results in decision-making. This reinforces the need for a segmentation framework living up to good segmentation criteria: Recognizable, stable and effective.

Addressing Challenge Three – How to drive sales and marketing effectively

Many sales and marketing activities are beyond the reach of impact studies – at least in executives' measures of results.

This is because marketing works at the early phases of the customer decision process by driving branding and customer communications to increase awareness. To explore this challenge, let's look at the AIDA model (Figure 2.6):

- A – Awareness/Attention: Attract the attention of the customer and make them aware of the firm's existence.

- I – Interest: Raise customer interest by demonstrating features, advantages and benefits.

- D – Desire: Convince customers that they want and desire the product or service and that it will satisfy their needs.

- A – Action/Acceptance: Lead customers towards taking action, i.e. purchasing from the firm.

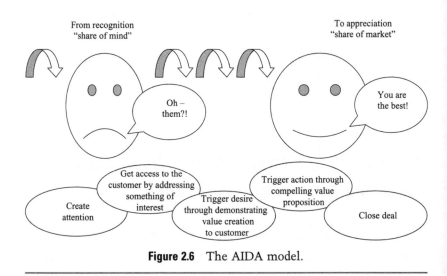

Figure 2.6 The AIDA model.

There are a few items to keep in mind:

- Firms do not live off of mind share but only of market share, i.e. results. Thus, executives are interested in creating market share. They know that higher mind share leads to higher market share but the dropout rates (i.e. the difference between the two figures) are so large that executives doubt any real correlation.

- Many firms have a mind share of nearly 100% in their market: Who does not know Coca-Cola, McDonald's, BMW and the like? In these firms, sales and marketing approaches for working with mind share are bound to irrelevance in the executive boardroom.

Few firms have sufficient customer and market insights to reveal the needs of their customers and, thus, to proactively drive customers to the action stage. Firms typically steer through the rear-view mirror based on tracking data and data from customer satisfaction reviews. Thus, they know what happened but have no means to set an agenda which makes an impact in the future. Most firms would like to be market leader but miss the customer insight to effectively move customers through the AIDA process. Still they say: If only we knew what's on the minds of our customers.

A good segmentation framework must cope with the third challenge by providing insights into what's on the minds of the customers. It must take the tacit customer knowledge held by the customer-facing employees of the firm and make it explicit. It follows that a good segmentation framework must provide a common language for harvesting, structuring, sharing and leveraging upon the most valuable asset of the firm, namely its customer knowledge. Equipped with this common language, executives and marketing and sales will have the foundation to systematically, effectively and efficiently work together on successfully leading customers through the AIDA funnel. This supports the notion of impact but also the notion of recognition and stability.

Towards the CUBEical Thinking business management framework

The internally focused management concepts developed and widely implemented during the last decades have been the vehicles for firms to minimize the resources allocated to and spent on a given activity or series of activities constituting subprocesses or complete business processes. Thus, BPR, JIT, lean, outsourcing, Six Sigma, ERP, CRM have been the means for firms to drive the resource efficiency through cost cutting. They are the means to drive EBITDA and value creation vis-à-vis their shareholders with a resource perspective.

Focusing on resource efficiency is about optimizing the resources spent on activities or business process, for example having an employee send as many promotion letters per hour as possible. BPR, lean, JIT and ERP systems are, in this regard, definitely helpful concepts in optimizing the resource efficiency, in bringing transparency to what is going on and in following up on performance over time. Alternatively, outsourcing is an option. As such, optimizing the resource efficiency and cutting costs will – everything else being equal – increase EBITDA.

Is such a one-sided optimization of EBITDA worth the effort? Yes definitely! If the promotion letters are to be sent out anyway, and nobody cares about how the receivers of the letters react to them, optimizing the resource efficiency will at least minimize the bottom-line damage associated with sending the letters out. But if firms do think of the receivers' reaction to the letter, the focus changes from resource efficiency to market efficiency. What if a firm wants to optimize not only letter production but also letter impact?

Not surprisingly, firms increasingly become aware of significant profit opportunities along the market efficiency axes. But firms also recognize the lack of a business management framework to develop this dimension – a framework which is well suited to the executives' requirements of context, accountability and results.

In response to this demand, we have developed the CUBEical Thinking business management framework. As we will unfold in the following three chapters, CUBEical segmentation makes the customer the pivotal point on the executive agenda for driving EBITDA because it lives up to good segmentation criteria and, thus, to executive requirements. Based on the insights provided by CUBEical segmentation, executives together with their customer-facing employees can start working on optimizing their market efficiency by outlining marketing, sales and new product development activities. Together with their colleagues from other functional areas, they can work on optimizing EBITDA by balancing market and resource efficiency. Thus, with CUBEical segmentation the new mantra of firms will be:

By leveraging on the customer insight provided by our CUBEical segmentation, we can optimize our customer relationships by adapting production and logistics, procurement and administration. Herewith, we improve our EBITDA result and achieve profitable revenue growth.

When unfolding the CUBEical segmentation framework in Chapter 3, we will explore current segmentation practice to understand how CUBEical segmentation wipes out current shortcomings. In Chapter 4, we document our way of profiling customers by defining customer types – capturing the relevant differences of customer behavior. In Chapter 5, we finalize the CUBEical segmentation framework by introducing roles and scenes to describe the complexity of situations or occasions in which the firm meets its customers.

3

The challenges of current segmentation models

WHEN SPEAKING WITH SALES AND MARKETING PEOPLE, dissatisfaction about the currently used segmentation model is a popular topic. It is just like discussing the weather in the UK – always a welcomed topic, everybody has an opinion, no one is really happy and everybody claims to have no influence whatsoever. What might be a reasonable conclusion for the weather is not acceptable regarding segmentation, i.e. regarding the structured understanding of a firm's customers. Someone must have developed and someone must have approved the currently used segmentation model for implementation.

The usual sources of dissatisfaction are:

- People cannot remember the segment descriptions: Segments are described in obscure terms that one needs to read over and over again to understand and remember what these segments are all about.

- Even if they can remember the segment descriptions, people have problems with assigning a customer to a given segment: The descriptions are so far away from real life – or based on unobservable items – that it becomes impossible to put a given customer in the defined boxes.

- Once in a box, people claim that the dynamics of the market make customers crawl out of the box again and into another one – or even that the boxes need relabeling every now and then.

- If the above hurdles are taken, people claim that the segments do not really make sense in terms of treating customers differently: Regardless of the box, customers behave differently anyway and no sales and marketing implications can be drawn.

All these sources of frustration lead firms to develop new segmentation models every now and then which are met by the organization with the BOHICA effect: *bend over, here it comes again.* As the last segmentation did not work, why bother with trying the new one? It has become fashionable to complain about segmentation. And after a few rounds of new segmentation models, no one can tell if failure is due to the segmentation model or the lack of implementation. Perhaps it is the mistake of the customers as they do not behave as the segmentation models dictate they should. Something is rotten in the state of segmentation!

Let's recall the criteria of good segmentation developed in Chapter 2:

- Customer segments must be intuitively recognizable. If not, the executives and customer-facing employees cannot differentiate between customers and a business strategy based on differentiation among customers will fail in its development and in its implementation. Segmentation must capture the real context of a customer in order to be understandable and manageable.

- Customer segments must be stable with regard to segment membership. If not, customers will be in one segment at one time and in another segment at another time. Which differentiation strategy should then apply? Furthermore, if segment membership is not stable the segmentation cannot support knowledge sharing and leveraging the organization's joint customer knowledge.

- Customer segments must be effective in the market by reflecting the needs and expectations of the customers: If not, actions taken by the firm based on the segmentation make no sense to customers and thus implementation of the firm's strategy has no impact on revenues.

Before we introduce CUBEical segmentation it is worth taking a look at some commonly used segmentation models and analyzing how well they fit these criteria in order to fully understand the need for a new segmentation framework.

Current segmentation models' fit to good segmentation criteria

Firms use a zillion different segmentation models – so it is not possible to review them all here. Rather, we have selected the most common ones – and even though your firm's segmentation model has a different name or is specially developed for your firm, some of your model's dimensions probably fit one of the following descriptions.

No-no segmentation

Some firms have yet to discover that customers are different. They see no need for segmentation. Obviously, their non-existing segmentation does not live up to any of the criteria for good segmentation.

These firms live in their internal orientation and market their products in a post-war manner: If only we have good products, customers will buy them. Prices are typically found on a cost-plus-profit basis as any insight into customers' value creation is missing. Members of this club are typically process technology companies (those who cannot change production for differentiating goods and services) and high-tech firms (those whose goods and services are technologically leading thus having a quasi-monopoly).

These firms consider their customers undifferentiated and are thus hard to convince of the need for customer segmentation. And those profitable firms which have enough customers without thinking of them are also hard to reach. There is no urge for introducing a good segmentation practice. Apparently such firms have not yet felt the heat of competition.

ABC segmentation

The first insight into different customer behavior is often provided by the accounting department as they are the ones who can calculate how much customers are buying and/or how profitable customers are. Typically, the volume and/or profit dimensions are combined in the ABC customer ranking – based on either current numbers or future potential. Combining volume and profit makes the categorization more solicited (Figure 3.1). Being below average in volume and/or profit margin normally implies that the customer is not important to the firm. Depending on the business model, small customers with high margins and large customers

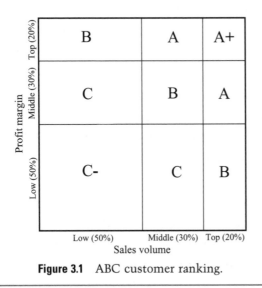

Figure 3.1 ABC customer ranking.

with low margins may be regarded as A customers. Surely, those with high volume and high margins are the superstars, A plus. Those with low volume and low margins (read: negative contributions) are the losers, C minus, who should be considered as potential candidates for contract cancellation.

The exact numbers for assigning customers to the three categories are firm specific but there is a preference for assigning the top 20% of customers to category A, the next 30% to category B and the rest to category C. The ABC groups do come with different titles in different firms: Some call their groups bronze, silver and gold with platinum as A plus; others use account, key account and strategic account with partnership account as the star category (there is a bit of variation whether "key" is higher than "strategic"); and some subscribe to junior, regular and senior accounts. Regardless of the specific naming convention used, the logic is the same.

One of the widespread misinterpretations of ABC customer ranking is that it is regarded as customer segmentation. But it is not as ABC customer ranking is based on internal characteristics and by no means on customer behavior. In our terms ABC ranking is really about portfolio management rather than segmentation. Firms segment their customers in terms of customers' importance to the firm and disregard the firm's importance to the customer (Figure 3.2). We call this the *perspective trap*.

Of course, focusing on the value a customer provides to the firm is necessary in order to secure profitability. Much harm can be done to a firm by allocating resources to unprofitable customers. As such, it is natural to conduct an ABC customer

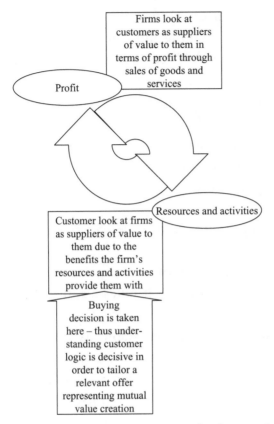

Figure 3.2 Two perspectives in mutual value creation.

ranking in order to discover financial differences once customers have been segmented into somewhat homogeneous
groups. However, ABC customer ranking cannot serve as the
basis for marketing and sales communication or product
development. It is not advisable to tell a customer that he or
she is classified as an A customer based on profitability
because such information will only result in demands for
lower prices by the customer.

ABC customer ranking does not answer the question: If only
we knew what is on our customers' minds. Instead, it is about

the minds of the firms serving the customers. The segments of ABC customer ranking link nicely to accountability and result – this is why ABC customer ranking has no problems in entering the boardroom. However, it does not give any means for strategy development and implementation. Everybody can state that having more A customers and fewer C customers is preferable, but we need insight into how to achieve this increased profitability for developing a strategy and for implementing it.

ABC customer ranking fails to deliver this part because:

- ABC customers cannot be intuitively recognized when interacting with them – it takes a spreadsheet;

- ABC membership is not stable as the whole rationale behind the ABC grouping is that customers, if feasible, should be moved from C over to B and further on to A based on increased sales and profits;

- ABC grouping has no market significance as sales or profits are reflecting the interests of the firm and, thus, not the needs and expectations of the customers.

The urge of most firms to differentiate themselves from competition by revealing customer needs and by setting customer expectations beyond the reach of competition cannot materialize with ABC grouping. The ABC grouping of customers is intended to help the firms plan their marketing, sales and new product development activities aimed at bringing customers to a higher level of volume or profits. Such plans will inevitably fail as long as customers within

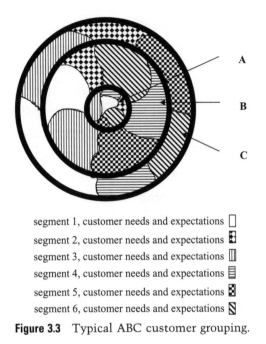

segment 1, customer needs and expectations ☐
segment 2, customer needs and expectations ⊠
segment 3, customer needs and expectations ⦀
segment 4, customer needs and expectations ☰
segment 5, customer needs and expectations ⊠
segment 6, customer needs and expectations ▧

Figure 3.3   Typical ABC customer grouping.

each of the ABC categories are inhomogeneous with respect to needs and expectations (Figure 3.3). For such campaigns, only bettors and gamblers can come up with an estimate on the market efficiency. Consequently, marketing most often turns to the only valid option; they communicate with customers in general terms and focus marketing on presenting product features rather than on presenting solutions the firm will bring to specific customers in specific situations.

No wonder that half of the sales and marketing budgets are spent without results – and no wonder that nobody knows which half. The result of the widespread use of ABC customer analysis, along with the tendency to forget about the underlying foundation and thus limitations in how the grouping can be utilized, has unintentionally derailed the discussion on segmentation.

Our experience is that most firms using ABC customer grouping are aware of its limitations but suppress their knowledge
of its inadequacy to provide valuable customer insights. The
usual saying is: "We have to start somewhere" and "it is
better than nothing". Yes, it is good that these firms are beginning to explore customer differences. And yes, customer profitability analysis is very important. In terms of moving forward
towards better customer insight, these firms are ready to
implement a new segmentation framework living up to the
requirements of good customer segmentation once they see
how it works and adds value.

Demo-firmo-graphic segmentation

Realizing the lack of customer insight, some firms have taken
the step of describing their customers using variables belonging to the customer in addition to ABC customer analysis.
The easiest way to accomplish this is of course to start with
something already registered in the CRM system. Many firms
describe their customers with demographics (B2C) and on
firmographics (B2B). Typically, parameters used for the
consumer include age, sex, disposable income, postal code,
and education level; for the business customer number of
employees, turnover, postal code, industry codes, sales, profits,
etc. are commonly employed.

Demo-firmo-graphic segmentation unfortunately opens the
door for the *registration trap* – the uncritical use of data
already registered and available inside the firm. The assumption is that "something" of relevance, one way or the other,
can be derived from data already at hand. The shortcut to

customer segmentation is to group customers around the demographic or firmographic characteristics which are used when registering transactions with the customers.

Unfortunately, these "perfect measures" rarely correlate with customer behavior and, thus, are unrelated to the AIDA process. Thus, this method of segmenting customers is not in line with good segmentation practice as it has no market effect. Databases of firms are predominantly filled with information represented by numbers which might be useful for other parts of the organization but not for sales and marketing. Much has improved in firms regarding the availability of customer-related data due to the increasing use of CRM systems – but there is still a gap between the information registered in a database and the knowledge useful for segmentation. What kind of car can we sell to a 35-year-old male with disposable income of $40000 for this purchase? We need to know what is on the customer's mind in relation to cars – sporty and esteemed, practical and economical, ecological, etc. Thus, even though the segments might be recognizable, demo-firmo-graphic segmentation lacks effectiveness.

Similarities between customers can sometimes be related to demographics and firmographics but the logic and order of the two steps is important: Customers within a segment are identified by their observable, recognizable behavior and then described with, for example, demographics and not the other way around. For example, a bank groups their customers by attitudes to overdraft, credits and preferred mode of interaction (personal vs internet banking) by using postal code, as market research suggested that differences in attitudes vary significantly by region. Thus, postal code is a very effective segmentation variable which is easy to assign as well. But understanding customers' behavior comes first. In this case postal code is only useful because it explains behavior. But more often, postal code has no relation to customer behavior!

Being short of alternatives, many firms stick to their demographic and firmograhic segmentation for the simple reason that they see some kind of link between the segments and the goods and services supplied. So it is better than nothing – and at least they can state that they segment their customers. Because these firms typically have many customers, they have automated customer segmentation. These firms generally know that their segmentation says nothing about what's on their customers' minds and they know that the fortunes spent on tracking customers and sales cannot be linked back to segmentation in a meaningful way. Consequently, if a manageable framework for good customer segmentation pops up they are ready to invest in an implementation hoping eventually to trace customers and sales better than with their existing demo-firmo-graphic segmentation.

Campaign segmentation

Firms employing campaign segmentation typically stick to demo-firmo-graphic customer data but instead of segmenting customers they are kept unsegmented in a database from which customers are picked and grouped on an ad hoc basis when running a specific marketing campaign. Selecting customers to be addressed through the campaign is hereby based on demographics (for consumers) or firmographics (for business customers) but it is assumed that the target group for the communication must be identified on a case-by-case basis through a given combination of customer characteristics fitting the purpose of the campaign. As such, these firms understand that customers need to be understood more differentiated than with the one-segment-assignment-fits-all-purposes approach, typical for demo-firmo-graphic segmentation.

But by all means, this way of segmenting has little to do with customer segmentation; it is merely a way to get some addresses or telephone numbers in order to send some sort of communication. Customers are not seen in their totality but as the recipients of messages. Thus, customers are grouped on an ad hoc basis and this creates a fragmented customer picture – which is unstable, not recognizable and only randomly effective.

In realizing that campaign segmentation is about finding recipients for marketing messages, to avoid overstretching the customers' letterboxes and telephones, customers are tagged every time they, for some reason, are being picked out for a campaign. Hereby, despite the fact that the firm assumedly finds their communication valuable to the customer, if a customer too often falls into the target group for communication, communication can be halted.

From our experience, firms working with campaign segmentation are fully aware that their segmentation practice is basically a dead-end street. They know that if they become even better in the discipline of data mining no real customer insight can be gained. Customers are merely a number to which some demographic or firmographic information, as well as some transaction data, is attached. Given the keys to good customer segmentation, these firms realize the great potential in building real customer insights. They are very open to solutions which bring together the fragmented customer pieces.

Realizing the shortcomings of demo-firmo-graphic-based segmentation practices, new segmentation practices have been tested during the recent years. One of these approaches builds on segmenting customers along archetypes, while the other approach builds on segmenting customers around different situations and occasions.

Archetype segmentation

Over the past 10 years, archetype segmentation is increasingly discussed and used. The basic notion is the development of some normative, stereotypical behaviors which span the maximum differences of customer behavior. To exemplify this, archetype food customers could, for example, be the "gourmet" and the "junk food freak". Such archetypes are easily recognizable and of market significance as the segments relate to consumer behavior. What about the stability of segment membership? Here, the turmoil gains momentum; "gourmets" eat junk food and the "junk food freaks" eat gourmet food, so archetype membership is unstable. The same customer may belong to different archetypes or be a mixture and combination of archetypes. This violates the stability requirement of good segmentation, hereby limiting its usefulness. And it actually violates the recognition requirement, too: We can recognize the archetype but not as a real customer.

The idea of archetype segmentation is great as it takes its departure in customer behavior. The improvement needed is to replace the normative, idealized behavior with real customer behavior. The aim is that each customer has only one type – we refer to this as "customer type" in CUBEical segmentation and explain the profiling process of identifying such types in Chapter 4.

The jumping back and forth between archetypes is often explained by the fact that the customer is in different situations while acting according to different archetypes. So let's look at this other recent trend of occasional and situational segmentation.

Occasions and situations

In our dynamic environment, the entire world might be too large to focus on for real understanding to occur. Therefore, firms have started to dissect customers into situations, also called occasions. The idea is to focus on a limited situation and work within it. For food and beverage firms, typical situations are a restaurant visit, a barbecue with friends, or a cinema visit. Such segmentation offers a clarity and sharpness which is very good. However, problems arise by cutting customers into pieces and not putting them together again – just like with campaign segmentation. But the customer is one whole creature – and puts these different situations together well. For a CEO whose firm enjoys preferential treatment with a bank as it makes thousands of transactions a year, standing in a queue for making a private transaction does not create satisfaction.

Another problem of situational segmentation models is that the list of situations is rather long. Regarding different shopper situations, i.e. different circumstances a customer encounters within a retail outlet, the market research firm AC Nielsen operates with over 30 different "missions" according to their website. All of these missions have logic behind them but the sheer number is hard to handle. Additionally, many situational segmentation models feature situations which are overlapping: Is "barbecue with friends" part of "eat at home" or are these two situations meant to be different? Is "cinema" different from "out with friends"?

What is needed is a framework to explain different situations while at the same time holding them together. This is achieved by explaining situations in terms of *roles* and *scenes* – further described in Chapter 5.

Situational segments are easily recognizable and of market significance, but segment membership is unstable as customers typically move through several occasions. Within these occasions, say a dinner at friends, general customer behavior cannot be explained as needs and expectations vary depending on whether it is a "gourmet" or a "junk food freak" attending the dinner.

These two trends in customer segmentation, archetypes and situations, discussed above have unintentionally catered to the prevailing perception in academia and practice that customers are moving targets. Consequently, this leads some to believe that improving segmentation is a mission impossible or that segmentation is an ongoing exercise where the segmentation framework employed has to be constantly modified in order to account for the turmoil characterizing customers. Most firms working with archetypes and situations/occasions are continuously searching for the right segmentation practice because they are aware of the problems.

The paradox is that the widespread perception of customers as moving targets and all the turmoil created by this view has little to do with customers. The paradox can be traced back to the endeavor of improving customer segmentation without properly addressing the criterion for good segmentation regarding stable segment membership. Herewith, the attempts made to improve segmentation practice have unintentionally derailed the discussion on customer segmentation.

No wonder customers are considered as moving targets. The segmentation framework itself makes the customer walk in and out of the segments represented by archetypes or occasions. Hence, customer behavior becomes highly unstable by default. Furthermore, as needs and expectations of customers cannot be explained in a stable model based on archetypes or occasions, customer loyalty seems not to exist or at least to be purely accidental.

But our research shows that customers can be loyal. Customer behaviors are highly stable and predictable over time and loyalty can be built provided a firm understands its customers. What the above discussion exemplifies is that if one or more of the three criteria of good customer segmentation are left out, the segmentation model is of limited business value (Figure 3.4).

Introducing CUBEical segmentation

Without a good segmentation framework there is no platform geared for harvesting, structuring, sharing and leveraging upon the most valuable asset of the firm – the knowledge about customers. This has created frustration for marketing

Criteria for good segmentation	How to...	Avoid...	If not...
Intuitively recognizable	Involve customer-facing employees in segmenting customers. See the world from the customers' perspective and only thereafter prioritize resources based on customers' profitability.	Avoid reliance on general databases and highly complex segmentation frameworks.	If not, the firm remains internally focused and undifferentiated to customers.
Stable	Look for underlying dimensions and typical behaviors and decision-making patterns.	Avoid segments changing all the time. Avoid short-term, small solutions which need to be redone soon.	If not, segmentation contributes to confusion and instability. If not, customer knowledge cannot be leveraged upon.
Effective	Think of what really matters for customers, what really makes customers buy or not, what really bothers customers.	Avoid internal view where customers are targeted solely based on the value created to the firm.	If not, all marketing resources are spent with random success and most resources are wasted.

Figure 3.4 The do's and don'ts in customer segmentation.

departments as they, in contrast to sales, only have sporadic face-to-face contact with customers. Consequently, marketing departments are the ones who have really been missing the common language which a good segmentation framework would provide as the vehicle for communicating across the firm about customer needs and expectations and about how to fulfill these. Thus, marketing has been left in a situation where they have had to rely on whatever information customer databases could bring about while striving to find new ways of segmenting customers in order to overcome the inadequacy of the current segmentation practices.

The urge for firms to be able to work with differentiated customer strategies reflects the fact that firms know that their customers differ with regard to their behaviors and ways of making decisions. Consequently, if it is feasible to segment customers according to their behavioral characteristics while fulfilling the characteristics of good customer segmentation, segmentation will be of business value.

Firms employ different segmentation models with a varying degree of customer insight (Figure 3.5). Developing the insights from archetype and situation segmentation further to fit the criteria for good segmentation, the fragmented images of customers need to form one clear picture. A picture in which the behaviors and ways of making decisions associated with one customer across different occasions are pulled together. As mentioned above, the lessons learned from the shortcomings of working with archetypes and situations are to work with customer types, roles and scenes. This segmentation framework is what we call the CUBEical segmentation framework (Figure 3.5 and 3.6).

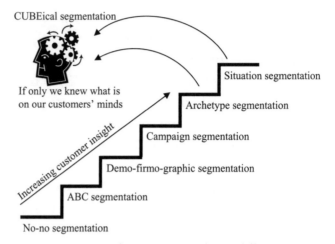

Figure 3.5 Customer insight staircase along different segmentation models.

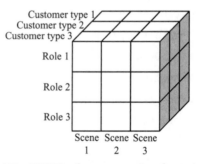

Figure 3.6 CUBEical segmentation framework.

CUBEical segmentation is the foundation for untying the Gordian knot hindering customers from becoming the pivotal focus on the executive agenda of driving profitable revenue growth as it provides the common language enabling the organization to communicate, share and leverage upon the customer knowledge of the firm. CUBEical segmentation is living up to the criteria for good customer segmentation both in full and in each of its parts; customer types will be described in Chapter 4 and roles and scenes will be described in Chapter 5. We will return to CUBEical segmentation in Chapter 6 where we look at the customer universe in its totality again.

4

Identifying customer types – inside the customer's mind

W HAT THE CUSTOMER HAS IN MIND WHEN THINKING about a good or service is the question to which executives and the customer-facing employees of the firm would like to have a structured answer. This knowledge helps a firm to reveal the foundation of true customer loyalty and it helps a firm to reveal the needs of its customers. Or to put it simply, this knowledge about customer minds is required for proactively setting customer expectation and gaining market leadership. Thus, answering the question offers an insight into unique business value.

Just consider the following examples.

Example 1

A consultancy offers advice to two professional farmers. The farmers are the same age, they both breed cattle and their economies are seemingly identical. Everything is the same –

acres of land, number of cattle, number of employees – and both are worried about the squeezed margins in the industry. Thus, their demographics are identical. The difference, however, is their type – their way of thinking about their businesses, reflected in their behavior and ways of decision-making. One farmer is a "developer", thinking "how can I grow my way out of the economic problems of this industry?"; the other is a "divester", thinking "how can I cash in and get out of the economic problems of this industry"? Consequently the interaction between the consultants and the two different customer types must be very different with regard to both value propositions and communications.

Example 2

One of our clients is a large distributor of industrial products, a complex business with many customers and a wide range of different products. In a business which was said to be dead a few years ago (we remember the slogan "cutting out the middle man"), this firm achieves 25% growth in turnover and profits year after year. Part of their success formula is customer insight. They realized that their customers bought from them for very different reasons, i.e. they were thinking differently when buying. One customer type is called "non-stopper": These customers are typically in the process industry, where production must run non-stop, 24 hours a day, 7 days a week, 365 days a year. Hence, these customers focus on operating hours – downtime is their worst enemy. A supplier to non-stoppers is part of these firms' optimization of their "operating hours" through equipment optimization and maintenance. A supplier creates value by prompt support in case of production breakdown through efficient, round-the-clock service concepts (24/7/365) and broadness and availability in their product portfolio.

Example 3

Think of consuming wine: Some customers just drink the wine, others taste it, look at the label, and talk at length about the taste of the wine, as well as the history of the producer. There are differences in the behavior of customers – and these differences do not correlate with demographics as there are young fellows with wine expertise and some older people who never had an interest in wine.

In searching for the answer, customer-facing employees typically explain that customers differ with regard to their behaviors and ways of making decisions. Furthermore, they contend that these variances make customers significantly different, as to both how a firm should interact with them and what sort of goods and services they are likely to buy.

When talking with sales people, who are the ones closest to the customer, they often use an intriguing language when discussing their customers. After a few sentences of description, they lean over and say: "You know that type, they always do that" or "It is that type of customer I really like".

So it is about customer types – types of real existing customers. Consequently, it is a straightforward idea to segment customers based on their type, i.e. their behavioral differences. Such segmentation will be of business value if it fulfills the criteria of good customer segmentation: Recognizable, stable and effective.

What is a customer type?

In a nutshell, a customer type is a description of one significant style of customer behavior and of making decisions when interacting with the firm in question. The description illustrates the key items of differentiation for the customer in question. As such, customer types are not anthropological accounts of every breath a customer takes. They never fill more than one Powerpoint slide – and are preferably between four and seven sentences long. Each customer type gets an expressive name for easy identification.

Figure 4.1 shows a customer type description of a farmer with an impulsive developer spirit, as mentioned above in Example 1.

While knowledge about the customer mind ("if only we knew what's on the mind of our customers") can be considered

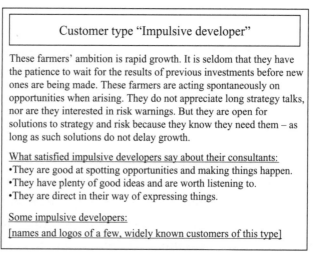

Customer type "Impulsive developer"

These farmers' ambition is rapid growth. It is seldom that they have the patience to wait for the results of previous investments before new ones are being made. These farmers are acting spontaneously on opportunities when arising. They do not appreciate long strategy talks, nor are they interested in risk warnings. But they are open for solutions to strategy and risk because they know they need them – as long as such solutions do not delay growth.

What satisfied impulsive developers say about their consultants:
•They are good at spotting opportunities and making things happen.
•They have plenty of good ideas and are worth listening to.
•They are direct in their way of expressing things.

Some impulsive developers:
[names and logos of a few, widely known customers of this type]

Figure 4.1   Example of a typical customer type description.

tacit knowledge held by the customer-facing employees of the firm, the customer type description is making this knowledge explicit by describing the associated customer behaviors and ways of making decisions in terms which everybody can recognize and act upon. Hereby, a common language for communicating about customers is established.

Values and beliefs in the customer minds drive individuals' behaviors but cannot be observed directly. People's behaviors exemplify both conscious and unconscious values and beliefs. We cannot see into people's and organizations' minds, it is hard to measure their values and beliefs. In comparison, we can observe, report and discuss actual behaviors and ways of making decisions – and we can categorize these into different customer types. What a customer considers being right or wrong (the customer's values and beliefs) are the key drivers for his or her behaviors decisions, and performance (Figure 4.2). Of course, the underlying reasons for customers' behaviors are important to understand.

In our research, customer-facing employees can easily describe and make their knowledge explicit about the middle part, i.e. the customers' behaviors and ways of making decisions. Therewith, they mirror their tacit knowledge about the

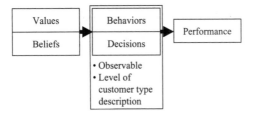

Figure 4.2 Linking the customer mind to customer behavior.

non-observable values and beliefs of customers into understandable and transferable descriptions. Thus, it makes no sense to try to identify values and beliefs; what matters for understanding customers is fully embedded in the customer type descriptions.

As a segmentation variable, customer type is in line with the characteristics of good customer segmentation:

- Customer types are by nature intuitively recognizable as they represent the way the customer-facing employees group customers according to their differences in their daily work.

- Customer types are by nature stable in the long term with respect to segment membership because customer behavior and ways of making decisions are mirroring the long-term stable values and beliefs of the individuals.

- Customer types enable market effectiveness as the customer behaviors and ways of making decisions are determining how the interactions between the customer and the firm unfold in the various occasions in which they meet.

Through employing customer types, CUBEical segmentation wipes out the shortcomings of existing segmentation practices. The notion of customer type radically breaks with the widespread perception in academia and practice of customers being moving targets. Customer types manifest the stability of customer behaviors and ways of making decisions. They are easily recognizable and have market

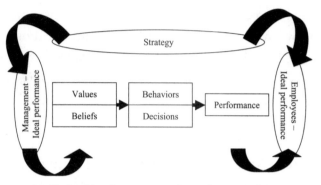

Figure 4.3 Corporate culture framework.

effect. In short, they fulfill all three criteria of good customer segmentation.

Interestingly, Figure 4.2 represents exactly the same framework which has been used during recent years for identifying and anchoring the corporate culture programs across organizations (Figure 4.3). Thus, customer types apply both to individual profiles as well as to organizational profiles. Consequently, our customer type framework is applicable for B2C as well as B2B markets.

Customer types driving true customer loyalty and branding effectiveness

Having been employed to guide corporate culture programs, the direct link between values and beliefs on one side and the manifestation of these in behaviors and ways of making decisions on the other side is by no means new to academia and practice. The puzzling truth is that the internal business focus characterizing recent decades has been so strong that the parallel between corporate values and customer values has been overlooked despite the many corporate value programs. It is the link between the two sides, a firm's values and beliefs and a customer's values and beliefs, which is the foundation for true customer loyalty that all firms try to achieve.

Corporate culture initiatives have aimed at aligning the organization around a strong common understanding of values and beliefs. The work on pinning down and anchoring the values and beliefs in firms has been implemented under slogans such as "Living our culture", "Living our values" or "One face to the customers". Artifacts of corporate culture in today's firms are found on badges, in receptions and cantinas, and on their websites. The logic behind these initiatives is: If management, in everything they do, refers back to the values and beliefs of the firm, the employees will start to behave and make decisions in line with these. Employees' behaviors and ways of making decisions gradually get aligned with the values and beliefs of the organization. If successful, the behavior and decision-making of employees is aligned and consistent. Corporate culture and strategy are thereby two sides of the same coin as the strategy defines target performance and culture defines the accepted way of getting there.

What is directly important to a customer is not the strategy of a firm, nor its values and beliefs as such. What a customer notices and responds to is the employees' behaviors and ways of making decisions. When customers are asked to give their view of a firm they are dealing with, they typically describe the employees' behaviors and the way of making decisions. Likewise, when the firms look at their best customers, what they see is not the customer's strategies, nor their values and beliefs – but their behavior and ways of making decisions.

Thus, when an individual finds the behaviors of another individual sympathetic and when the two individuals' ways of making decisions are aligned and transparent, the two are sharing values and beliefs within the sphere of interaction. Therewith, the foundation for true loyalty is laid. Likewise if customers of a given customer type find the behaviors of a firm sympathetic and when the two parties are sharing the same patterns of decision-making, the foundation for true loyalty is present. Thus, it is by aligning the firm's behaviors and decision-making process vis-à-vis the behaviors and decision-making processes of customers of a given customer type that true customer loyalty is generated.

Hereby, the notion of customer types is breaking new ground in linking CUBEical segmentation directly to the concept of customer loyalty. Customers of a given customer type with whom the firm already has strong relationships are the ones with whom they share values and beliefs. Thus, the behavior of the firm is aligned with the behavior of the customer and the mutual decision-making processes work smoothly. Consequently, true loyalty prevails and the widespread perception of customer instability is misplaced.

Corporate culture programs often have the objective of showing "one face to the customer". Actually, the same objective was spelled out for the customer relationship management initiatives, of which there were many during the recent decade.

Paradoxically, the "one face to the customer" intention is inconsistent with the view that customers are different and consequently should be served in different ways, i.e. with different behaviors. We need "one face to one customer" (customer consistency) but also "different faces to different customers" (customer diversity). The introduction of customer types adds value to the corporate culture programs by explicitly offering the opportunity to map both sides of values and beliefs against each other and, thus, translating a firm's own values into customer values. While a firm's values and beliefs do not match 100% with all customer types, the overlap must be sufficiently strong to secure true customer loyalty.

The work on anchoring corporate values of the organization among the employees is most often followed by a corporate and product branding campaign. To strengthen and maintain customer relationships, these branding initiatives aim at providing customers with insights into the firm's values and beliefs. Such endeavors can only succeed if the customer types are identified. Firing messages of corporate values into the open air has a great potential of not hitting the target. The notion of customer types brings clarity to corporate and product branding through the insight into how the individual customer types perceive the value creation by the firm. Based on this insight, the performance of corporate and product branding can be increased significantly by knowing customer types.

Let's consider an example: An industrial distributor had developed a set of customer values aimed at explaining to customers and employees what the firm stands for in their markets

(Figure 4.4). The introduction of these customer values had a tremendous positive impact – internally. For customers, these four values were too abstract. Thus, the firm began to analyze what their values actually meant for the different customer types and accordingly translated the values, first into features and then into a customer perspective. Customers now understand why the firm is the right partner for

Firm's aim	Customers do not need to shop elsewhere – the firm is the one-stop-shop solution provider			
Firm's promise	All the products needed, at competitive prices and quality, made available in an easy and efficient way.			
Firms overall customer values	Complete	Competitive	Quality experience	Easy and efficient
Value features (how the firm supports the values)	Wide product portfolio Product as well as know-how and consulting	Price/offering Concepts that make our customers more competitive	Personnel quality Product quality Delivery quality	Easy ordering Nearby collection points 24-hour service Efficient supply chain management
Customer translation to non-stopper	This firm has all the goods and services to make our production run	This firm provides suggestions for new goods and service which further minimize our downtime	This firm is part of our systematic high quality maintenance	This firm is close and quick when needed
Customer type: Non-stopper	These customers are typically in the process industry, where production must run non-stop, 24 hours a day, 7 days a week, 365 days a year. Hence, these customers focus on operating hours – downtime is worst enemy.			

Figure 4.4 Value translations.

long-term relationships. Internally, the substrategies for the different customer types are bound together as they are connected to the overall customer values.

How to identify customer types?

Being the ones closest to customers, it is a paradox that sales people are not often mobilized to give their input to segmentation and that they accept living with what others develop for them. General management and marketing underestimates the importance and value of the customer knowledge held by sales people. It is a widespread perception that sales people have a too pragmatic and short-sighted view of customers. Why people with limited, if at all, customer contact are better suited to segment customers is a question so far unanswered. And every firm has customer-facing employees – otherwise it is a miracle how customers get their goods and services and pay for them. Workshops with the customer-facing employees generally work fine for identifying customer types both for B2B and B2C firms (option 1 in Figure 4.5).

But sometimes, firms need to segment customers further down the value chain and, thus, may not have access to people with direct customer contact. Also, when direct customer interaction is very sporadic and customer knowledge inside the firm is very limited a different identification process has to be employed. Whatever the reason for not using customer-facing employees, we also describe an identification process with direct customer input via focus groups and surveys (option 2 in Figure 4.5).

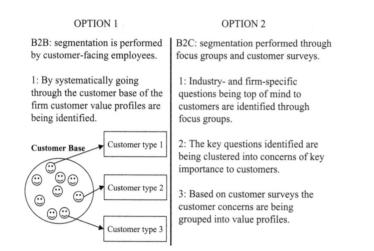

OPTION 1

B2B: segmentation is performed by customer-facing employees.

1: By systematically going through the customer base of the firm customer value profiles are being identified.

OPTION 2

B2C: segmentation performed through focus groups and customer surveys.

1: Industry- and firm-specific questions being top of mind to customers are identified through focus groups.

2: The key questions identified are being clustered into concerns of key importance to customers.

3: Based on customer surveys the customer concerns are being grouped into value profiles.

Figure 4.5 Identification options for customer types.

Thus, there are two ways to identify customer types – workshops with customer-facing employees or focus group interviews in combination with customer surveys. From our experience, option 1 works fine in nine out of 10 cases. Consequently, whenever feasible we recommend option 1 of involving customer-facing employees. Even when firms need to segment customers further down the value chain, we recommend involving the customer-facing employees of the intermediaries as they are just as interested as the firm in driving profitable revenue growth.

Every now and then, we meet firms expressing the opinion that only data from customers can be correct data – something we don't subscribe to in general. What should be remembered is that customer needs may be unconscious for the customer. Also, expressing one's own behavior is difficult – how am I when going through a supermarket?

Option 1: Profiling performed by customer-facing employees

Sales people know their customers: They meet them on a regular basis face to face, phone to phone, and email to email. When asking sales people how customers differ they will exemplify this by describing how customers behave differently. They not only know customers' differences but also which of the differences are important.

Most firms have customers, with whom they have very good relationships, often reaching many years back in time. And most firms have at least a few good sales people that are recognized within the organization for having great customer insights. These are the sales people that should be selected for the workshops. Typically, between five to eight customer-facing employees are selected for the workshops. The number ensures variety but also leaves the opportunity for intensive discussions and enough time for everybody to be involved, heard and integrated.

Prior to the first workshop, the participants are asked to pick some of their best customers and to think about the relationship with regard to the customers' behaviors and their ways of making decisions. At the workshop the participants are individually asked to present their customers. Through a facilitated process, short half page descriptions of customer types are formulated exemplifying the significant behaviors of that customer. It is the rule not the exception that other participants will contribute to each others' descriptions because they have "the same type" in their own portfolio of customers.

Typically, the customer type description should cover the following points:

- Who are they?

- What characterizes them?

- What are their ambitions?

- What are they demanding?

- What do they appreciate about the way our firm is serving them?

- What are the do's and don'ts?

Once the discussion of one customer has been finalized, a new customer is picked. For every new customer the initial question to be asked is: Does the customer fit one of the customer types previously described or should a new customer type description be made? If a description is ambiguous for participants, i.e. they do not know whether or not a customer is of a certain type, the factors causing this ambiguity are identified and the customer type description is revised accordingly. By this iterative process, the descriptions are sharpened and the differences between customer types are discussed openly. By discussing other customers, the customer type descriptions are gradually being modified from describing the behaviors and ways of making decisions of one or a few customers to describing the behaviors and ways of making decisions of a wider group of customers belonging to the customer type in question.

Despite the general opinion that there must be many customer types, this process quickly reaches a stage where every new customer picked can be fitted into one of the customer types already described. From our experience with clients in different industries, the number of customer types usually ranges from four to eight, with a clear bias toward low numbers. As customer types are intuitively recognizable, participants start giving the customer types names – names which normally nicely depict the specific profile of these different types. The identification of customer types is completed when every customer picked from the customer database fits well into one of the customer type descriptions and when each of the customer types has a suitable name.

Once the segmentation is completed, the customer type descriptions should be finalized by identifying the three key statements which satisfied customers should tell their peers when talking about their relationship with the firm. These statements basically condense the foundation for true customer loyalty between the customers belonging to a customer type and the firm.

Even though the process is easy and straightforward, it normally takes three to five days to complete depending on customer diversity and participants' knowledge of customers. It is highly recommended to schedule the workshop days over a few weeks to allow reflection about the already developed customer type descriptions. Some of our participants have tested the increased insight between workshops – with the result of increasing revenue. There is no better way to roll out a new segmentation with already existing success stories.

Option 2: Profiling performed through focus groups and customer surveys

To identify customer types of a firm having sporadic face-to-face contact with customers or having limited knowledge of customers, focus groups and customer surveys can be employed. In focus groups, industry-specific top-of-mind concerns of customers are being identified: What are you thinking of when buying or consuming the goods and services of the firm? Hereafter, these concerns are sorted into groups of similar themes and issues.

These groups of concerns are then turned into questions for a questionnaire which a representative sample of customers will be asked to fill in. Processing the answers reveals a limited number of statistically significant clusters. Like option 1, the number of clusters is typically in the range of four to eight, with a clear bias towards low numbers.

Presenting the clusters by the underlying variables, employees of the firm can typically by intuition envisage, name and describe the customer types identified. Once the customer types are identified through the quantitative analysis, customer types are documented through short half page descriptions highlighting the significant behaviors and concerns. These descriptions normally benefit from focus group insights by using customers' own words and descriptions.

Testing customer types

The descriptions of the customer types are used across the organization as the common language and frame of reference for harvesting, sharing and leveraging upon customer knowledge in strategizing and executing. It is therefore important to carefully test the descriptions before they are introduced across the organization. We recommend that the segmentation is tested with another group of customer-facing employees, groups of employees in different departments with different degrees of customer knowledge, and at different hierarchy levels. This can be done by asking them to assign customers they know to the developed customer types. This is a comprehension test but also an effective way of looking for customers which for some reason do not fit in.

Another test is for completeness. To avoid a myopic view of customers, firms may think of their competitors and how their customers fit the customer type descriptions. Especially if a firm is highly specialized (niche firm), there is a small danger of overlooking some customer types only by working with existing customers. This test avoids this pitfall.

Assigning customers to customer types

With the customer types at hand, customer-facing employees are now ready – and from our experience highly motivated – to assign customer types to the remaining customers in the customer database. Due to differences in the numbers of customers and the customer insight held by the customer-facing employees, the assignment process is carried out in different ways.

With a smaller number of customers and high customer knowledge, assigning remaining customers is a straightforward exercise carried out by the customer-facing employees. For the customer-facing employees who have not been participating in the profiling workshops it takes only a half-day workshop to enable them to assign their customers according to customer type. This is the most precise assignment option as it is based on individual, knowledge-based assessments.

If customer knowledge is not available, an alternative option is the development of killer questions. Given the differences between customer types, it is possible to design a few questions which enable the assignment of a customer type to a customer. Customer-facing employees, e.g. people in sales, call centers, customer service, shop assistants, etc., get a script of killer questions and type the answers into the CRM system as soon as they receive them. A conference hotel chain operates with two killer questions segmenting customers into three types (Figure 4.6). This option can take quite some time before customer types can be fully implemented but the assignment is performed instantly when in contact with a customer and becomes a natural part of customer interactions. Killer questions are as precise as the first option.

Another option is the opportunity for self-assignment by customers. Firms can put leads out into their markets and let customers react to them. This is typically done via differentiated communications with tracking. Electronic newsletters

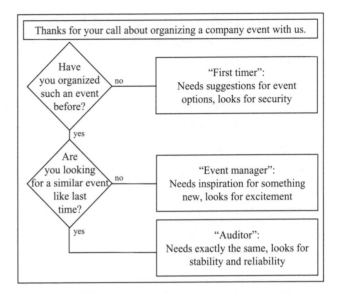

Figure 4.6 Killer questions for customer type assignment.

feature different stories which appeal to different customer types. By registering click-through behavior, customers can be assigned. Similarly, different telephone numbers and websites are used with TV advertisements. A telecommunication firm realized that only two out of five customer types visited their shops – a clear self-assignment effect which reduced the complexity of handling customers in their shops. This option is not as precise as the aforementioned ones but is very efficient with large numbers of customers.

Finally, available data which correlates significantly with customer types can be used to assign customer types. This method is rather imprecise as those variables registered in CRM databases (e.g. age, sex and postal codes – typical demo-firmographics) do rarely correlate well with customer types. But in spite of better sources, a good guess might be better than total

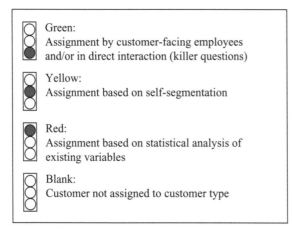

Figure 4.7   Assignment accuracy traffic light.

lack of assignment. Or in other words: Rather 50% wrong than 100% blind. The assignment accuracy can be put into the CRM system as a traffic light (see Figure 4.7).

Summing up customer types: why do customer types work?

For gaining relevance in the boardroom, we defined three criteria for good segmentation:

- Customer segments must be intuitively recognizable. If not, the executives and customer-facing employees cannot differentiate between customers and a business strategy based on differentiation among customers will fail in its development and in its implementation. Segmentation must capture the real context of a customer in order to be understandable and manageable.

- Customer segments must be stable with regard to segment membership. If not, customers will be in one segment at one time and in another segment at another time. Which differentiation strategy should then apply? Furthermore, if segment membership is not stable the segmentation cannot support knowledge sharing and leveraging the organization's joint customer knowledge.

- Customer segments must be effective in the market by reflecting the needs and expectations of the customers. If not, actions taken by the firm based on the segmentation make no sense to customers and thus implementation of the firm's strategy has no impact on revenues.

Attempts to improve segmentation practice by employing, for example, customer archetypes as a basis for segmentation have failed because the requirement of stable segment membership was ignored. This unintentionally led academia and practitioners to the conclusion that customers are moving targets. As a basis for segmenting customers, customer types are in line with the criteria of good customer segmentation:

- Customer types are intuitively recognizable as they represent the way the customer-facing employees experience customers in their daily work. They capture real customer differences and describe them in their own language.

- Customer types are stable over time and, thus, predictable. Customers, individuals and organizations do not easily change their values and beliefs – something every change management consultant and every new manager is aware of. As individuals, we do not change much: Those who were tardy in school still have trouble showing up on time. Human beings are rather predictable in their way of thinking about the world, their lives, and which goods and services may suit them well. Herewith, the notion of customer types breaks with the widespread perception of customers as moving targets. Customer types manifest the stability of customer behaviors and ways of making decisions.

- Customer types enable market effectiveness as the customers' behaviors and ways of making decisions are determining how the interactions between the customer and the firm unfold. As customer types capture the customer mind, they are close to the action and, thus, close to the interesting part of the AIDA model – the part where market share is created.

Without a good segmentation framework there is no platform for harvesting, sharing and leveraging upon the most valuable asset of the firm – the knowledge of customers. This has been frustrating for many but in particular for marketing as they only have sporadic face-to-face contacts with customers. Thus, marketing has been left in a situation where they have had to rely on inadequate customer insight for developing programs to influence the unknown.

From our research and our assignments with clients in B2B and B2C, the perception of customers being moving targets who are showing very vague traces of customer loyalty seems to be out of context. Customer behavior is highly stable over time and customer loyalty can be built provided the firm knows its customers. What the above discussion exemplifies is that segmentation is of limited business value when the three criteria for good segmentation are not fulfilled.

Revealing the customer types of the firm, no matter which method is being used, has a very strong impact on the performance of the customer-facing staff. The perceived change from being the one chasing customers as moving targets to being the one able to target customers is breaking down a mental barrier in handling customers and has a strong encouraging effect. It is the stability of the customer types that urges the employees to take an even more structured and proactive approach to sales and marketing than ever before. Basically nothing new has been invented – the effect simply comes from sorting out the customer knowledge already at hand in an intuitively understandable, easily recognizable, stable and market effective framework.

Customer types are descriptions summarizing the various behaviors and ways of making decisions. For developing customer types, our practice has revealed three key success factors:

- Involving customer-facing employees in the identification process is from our experience a key success factor for customer segmentation in both options. This involvement secures the recognition of the customer type descriptions, both content and language.

- Another key success factor is time. Both options need time to develop the right number and the right descriptions for the customer types. Rushing through it does not allow discussions to explore the similarities and differences sufficiently. Lack of time leads to a segmentation just like the old one – superficial, unrecognizable and having no market effect.

- The process is best supported with external moderation. Internal participants are often too bound to their existing segmentation and jump to conclusions too quickly – simply because they know the customers so well. A critical discussion of customers is most effectively achieved with external support – also because participants cannot get around difficult issues with "you know what I mean". The external moderators do not know, so tacit knowledge needs to be made explicit.

The notion of customer type is based on the general culture framework consistently linking together the values and beliefs, behaviors and decision patterns, and performance. By employing this framework we have demonstrated how the notion of customer types is breaking new ground in customer segmentation not only by living up to good segmentation practice but also by uniting segmentation of individuals and corporations into the same framework.

By fulfilling the requirements of good segmentation, the notion of customer types is of business value, meaning that the introduction of customer types into segmentation will make customers the pivotal focus on the executive agenda and, thus, drive profitable revenue growth. Hence, customer types are the foundation for creating true customer loyalty and for effective corporate branding, product branding and customer communication in general.

Is this the beginning and the end of the customer universe? Not quite. In the next chapter we need to solve another critical issue – the notion of situational needs and occasionally changing customer behavior within the universe.

5

Identifying roles and scenes – inside situations and occasions

WITH THE INSIGHTS PROVIDED BY SEGMENTING customers according to their customer type, the first step for generating profitable revenue growth is taken. Customer types explain the differences between *different* customers. But there is still variance in customer behavior which customer types cannot account for: The varying behavior of the *same* customer. So the challenge is only partially fulfilled, and partially still open: *If only we knew what's on the minds of our customers.*

With the customer type at hand, firms obtain insight into the foundation of true customer loyalty, i.e. the insight into how the firm must adapt its behaviors and decision patterns to those of the customers belonging to the different customer types. This enables the firm to secure a reasonable overlap between the values and beliefs of the firm vis-à-vis the values and beliefs of these customer types. This insight is a pre-requisite for building long-lasting profitable relationships. In order to gain full leverage from this insight firms must also have insight into where, with whom, and how the interactions with customers actually take place. Firms need to interact with their customers – it is through these interactions that business is created.

Taking a given customer type and asking the customer-facing employees about where, with whom and how they do business, they will start talking about the various situations in which they meet the customers in question. They will explain that the behaviors and ways of making decisions, as described for the customer type, unfold in different ways depending on the situation or occasion where the interaction takes place. Concerning a single customer, one key account manager stated: "This customer's production manager is easy going and accepts whatever we suggest when we meet on the shop floor while servicing the production equipment. But he is a real nightmare, going into ridiculous details when we have our yearly budget talks at his office." The same customer shows varying behavior in different situations – and a segmentation model must account for this.

From our assignments with clients we find it an interesting observation that the ambiguity of situations, one of the negative aspects of situational segmentation discussed in Chapter 3, does not exist for customer-facing employees. As outlined, they are very specific about where an interaction takes place, who they meet and how the customer behaves. In the example above, the key account manager meets the production manager in his role of being responsible for maintenance and the scene for the interaction is on the shop floor. In the second part of the example, the key account manager meets the production manager in his role of being responsible for negotiating the maintenance contract and the scene for the interaction is in his office. The ambiguity of situations has been wiped out by referring to the building blocks of the situation, i.e. role and scene for the customer interaction. Customer behavior varies with roles and scenes – not in a random fashion but in a manner where the behaviors and decision patterns for a given customer type are always exposed in the same predictable way in a given situation.

Sales people are used to meeting customers in different situations and they know that needs and expectations of customers differ across occasions. Sales people know that behaviors and decision-making patterns of a customer type are exposed in different ways depending on the situation, i.e. the sales people are not referring to the behavior of the production manager archetype in the one situation and to the archetype of the purchasing manager in the other situation. For them, a customer is one customer – nothing else makes sense to them. It is most unlikely that a sales person explains to the sales director that sales are going well with one archetype but not at all with another archetype. The customer is one account and the account manager intuitively caters for the complexity of the customers in the way they are being served. Thus, to be of business value, a segmentation model must mirror this complexity.

CUBEical segmentation is mirroring this way of thinking by using "real" customer types (not archetypes) and by using roles and scenes as the building blocks of situations and occasions where interactions with the customer take place.

Before exploring the link between customer type, roles and scenes, i.e. going into the customer universe, let's look in more detail at the decomposition of situations into roles and scenes.

What is a role?

Regarding customers as single-minded is usually a fatal mistake. Customers are multividuals, i.e. they perform different roles in their interaction with a firm.

Consider the following example: A woman arrives one morning at the airport as a "business traveler" having one set of needs for the service provided (e.g. good working conditions in the airport and in the aircraft). The next day the very same customer shows up with her family and in this mother-role, needs are quite different from those of the business traveler (e.g. children's playground and diaper changing facilities). Consequently, the actual role of the "multividual" defines differences in needs – the differences in the things that are on the customer's mind.

Roles are the specific relationships which a customer has vis-à-vis other people, e.g. friends and family in the private sphere or colleagues and managers in the business sphere. Even though customers frequently change between roles, the roles themselves are stable. Throughout history, there have always been these roles, e.g., spouse, parents, friends, colleagues, purchasing manager, and CEO. Roles are easily recognizable because we know them as we experience them in our own universe and because they have been around for a long time.

Roles are important because they, in combination with the customer type, determine customer needs. Thus, roles live up to the three criteria for good segmentation: recognizable, stable, and effective.

What is a scene?

Scenes are the customer touch points, where customers interact with a firm and/or its offerings. A scene is the environment in which the interaction takes place – the context of interaction. Again, scenes are not new territory in marketing – we are used to talking about marketplaces, market spaces in the digital world, space management and layout planning in retailing. We know that customer behavior is significantly influenced by the context of interaction. A common observation is the difference in customer behavior that occurs when meeting at the customer's office as compared to meeting at the supplier's office.

Scenes are easily recognizable:

- At home – with subcategories of at the dinner table, in the living room, etc.;

- At work – with subscenes of office, meeting room, shop floor, etc.;

- On the go – with subscenes of at the station, on the train, driving a car, etc.;

- In a shop – with subscenes of parking place, entrance area, different grocery departments, check-out point.

Of course, the relevant set of scenes and the level of detail (home vs living room) depends on a firm and its goods and products. But the scenes are stable, just like roles.

Creating new scenes is typically a matter of technological development and as such a matter of varying customer expectations. In this respect, the internet has brought major changes. For example, only a few years back in time, banking was something to be done between 10am and 4pm at the bank's branch (a scene). Today, most ordinary banking issues can be solved via the internet – and customers use the new tools at work or at home (the new scene for banking). Driven by technology, one scene has replaced another.

Scenes live up to the three criteria for good segmentation: They are recognizable, stable, and effective.

Customer universe and competitive arenas

Returning to the customer-facing employees' insights into situations, another interesting point arises: For a given customer type there is only a limited number of situations that are of importance to the customers belonging to the customer type. Thus, the link between customer type and relevance and importance of specific situations, i.e. combinations of roles and scenes, provides firms with a map of the customer universe for a given customer type.

Looking across the situations of relevance to a given customer type, e.g. customer type 1 in Figure 5.1, the two situations

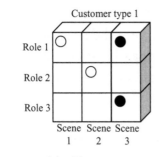

● = arena visited by customer type and important
○ = arena visited by customer type but not important
" " = arena not visited

Figure 5.1 Customer universe map: Competitive arenas for a customer type.

marked with a black dot are the important ones, the ones with a white dot are arenas which the customer visits but which are not very important for the customer. Those situations not marked at all are not visited by this customer type. This is either due to the infeasibility of these situations or because no firm addresses them, thus the customer has no opportunity to interact in these situations. The high and low importance situations make up the *customer universe for a given customer type* – pointing out all the situations in which the customers in question appear and where interactions with the firm take place or potentially could take place.

This mapping of the customer universe mirrors the experience seen through the eyes of the specific customer type. The interaction between the firm and the customer involves tailoring the marketing mix of the firm to address the specific needs of the given customer type in the specific situation. Consequently, the cubes in Figure 5.1 are *submarkets* where the firm competes against its peers for its share of the customer's wallet or alternatively the situations which the firm deliberately has decided not to address. We therefore denote these submarkets as the *competitive arenas* of the firm.

The notion of customer universe is important as it provides insights into what it takes to secure true customer loyalty vis-à-vis a given customer type. Thus, if the firm is not present or if it is not competitive within one of the competitive arenas of importance to a given customer type, space is left open for competitors to take over. For example, if only one hotel, one car rental, or one bank is represented in a town, a customer has no option other than to choose that offering. Thus, other hotel chains, car rental firms and banks give the local competitor a chance to promote its offerings to the customer beyond the given town. This is not to say that every hotel group needs hotels in all possible locations – but they need a hotel in every place important to their customers. Likewise, bank customers nowadays want access to their accounts whenever they need it. If a bank does not offer this service via the internet, i.e. does not feature in scenes other than at the branch, customers will defect.

Returning to the example in Figure 5.1, focus must be given to role 1 and role 3 as well as scene 3 because these roles and the scene combined cover the two competitive arenas of importance. As such, the customer universe map offers a tool for resource allocation for winning customer business and customer loyalty. If a firm is not able to position itself favorably in one subcube, the game is over for this particular competitive arena. As the customer oversees all competitive arenas in his or her universe, losing one competitive arena may have negative effects on winning other arenas. The connection between arenas is given by the importance of an arena to the customer – as previously mentioned, some arenas are of major importance for customers and failure to deliver potentially disqualifies a firm completely for this customer (the "black dot" fields in Figure 5.1). Other arenas are moderately important and not interacting in these arenas has potentially limited effects on the overall firm–customer relationship.

Firms generally do not have the resources to be in all arenas and thereby they have to rely on spillover effects from one arena to another. Based on a winning offer in one arena, a firm might convince customers to accept fewer competitive offers in other, less important arenas. This bundling of competitive arenas is usually done under the headings of "one-stop shopping", "single sourcing" and "total solutions" where the focus is put on the overall offering across the different competitive arenas.

To achieve profitable revenue growth, customers must have access to the firm and its goods and services. Only access to goods and service generates revenues and market share as opposed to mind share which only requires communication channels. Therefore, it is very important to understand the competitive arenas in which customers are experiencing the firm and its goods and services. We add the physical world to the CUBEical segmentation framework through roles and scenes to provide insight into the customer universe.

To interact in a positive atmosphere, customers must be within their comfort zones. On the one hand, customer-facing employees know from experience that switching scenes potentially can pull a customer out of the comfort zone. Consequently, such a move can jeopardize the relationship and business. On the other hand, customer-facing employees also know that a change in scenes sometimes opens up different dialogs and helps in solving problems, thus contributing to intensifying a business relationship. Firms are actively exploring new scenes for easing the atmosphere of interaction, e.g. golf tournaments, sponsored travel and product testing, or even joint marathon training.

Competitive arenas are important as a firm's insight into these provides the foundation for generating profitable revenue growth based on long-lasting relationships – based on stability, recognition and effect. This translates well into the executive requirements of context, accountability and results – thus making customers the pivotal focus on the executive agenda.

How to identify roles and scenes?

Relevant roles and scenes are as mentioned known within firms – it normally takes little time to identify the relevant roles and scenes. In principle, the identification options for roles and scenes are similar to the identification options for customer types.

Customer-facing employees

Similar to how it is for customer types, it is the customer-facing employees who hold the knowledge concerning the situations and occasions of importance in which interactions with customers take place. Therefore workshops with the customer-facing employees are the way forward for identifying the roles and scenes to be used in the firm's CUBEical segmentation framework.

Based on the customer-facing employees' day-to-day experience with customers, the first step in a systematic approach to identify roles and scenes is to make a list of the customer activities generally performed when interacting with the customer in question. Such activities are well known and intuitively recognizable to everybody in the firm and most often these activities are supported by streamlined business processes within the firm. Examples of activities could be:

- Seeking information;

- Requesting a proposal;

- Testing a product;

- Signing a contract;

- Ordering products;

- Receiving products;

- Paying bills;

- Receiving training, getting products installed;

- Handling maintenance and repair issues.

Once this activity cycle is determined, customer-facing employees can put scenes to the activities (where does it happen?) and identify roles of the people involved (who is acting?). Beyond the intuitive recognizable roles, a worthwhile systematic approach is to look at the customer activity chart as exemplified in Figure 5.2 and look for patterns of varying behavior. Parallel activities (i.e. customers do either one activity or another) normally point to different roles. Alternatively, activity chains can be divided into subchains corresponding to roles according to different timeframes or different purposes of the activities.

Take air transportation as an example (Figure 5.2). There is a significant difference in behaviors at the airport: Some go to the lounge and others visit the playground. Some read the newspaper and others a children's book. This is captured by assigning the roles, for example, "business person" and "parent". Looking at the activities, there is a pre-travel part of planning and booking and a travel part of flying. And there is a fair likelihood that these activities are not performed by the same people. As such, it makes good sense to assign a role, e.g. "planner", to differentiate from "traveler" – the traveler being subdivided into, for example, "business person" and "parent". For corporate clients, there are activities related to making a general contract and having yearly negotiations about it. Thus, there is a "contractor" role. Normally, roles do fall naturally into the customer activity chart – and customer-facing employees are excellent at pointing out what makes sense and what does not. But the example also highlights that the assignment of roles is industry- and firm-specific – what makes sense for one firm might not apply to another. So there is no short-cut – the process has to run in the firm.

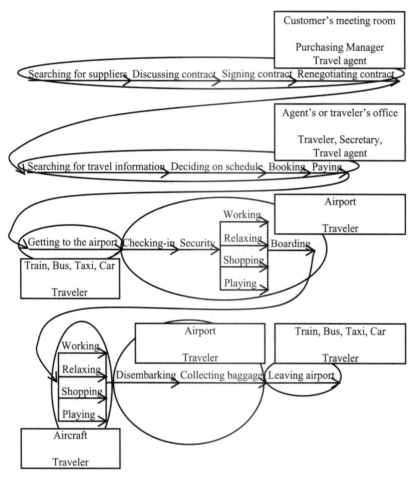

Figure 5.2 Customer activity chart for air transportation.

Customer experience analysis

In cases where either the access to customer-facing employees or their knowledge of customers is limited, input comes from customers directly. Focus groups are an option focusing on customers, describing their day-to-day activities and where these activities are performed. Alternatively, following customers through their day and observing their activities is also an option. As most firms' competitive arenas do not cover 24 hours for their customers, observations can be focused on the relevant activities or time spans. For retailers, observing customers while in their retail outlet might be sufficient. Analyzing call protocols in call centers might reveal the different roles of customers – i.e. what they had on their minds when calling. All of the information gained is used to build the customer activity chart and derive roles from it (Figure 5.3).

Summing up roles and scenes

In this chapter we finalized the discussion of the dimensions of CUBEical segmentation by adding the two dimensions roles and scenes to the framework. Together, roles and scenes make up the situations or occasions where customers interact with a firm. For a given customer type, the behaviors and ways of making decisions are exposed in different but predictable ways across the specific situations in which a firm meets the customers in question. These situations or occasions can be considered the submarkets or, as we denote them, the competitive arenas of the firm. It is in these arenas that a firm meets its peers and competes for the customer business.

For a given customer type, the firm can explore the customer universe by stepping into the different roles and understanding the different scenes from within. By linking together the competitive arenas of relevance and importance for a given customer type, the customer universe of a specific type is defined.

	Mon	Tues	Wed	Thurs	Fri	Sat	Sun
Breakfast							
Morning							
Lunch							
Afternoon							
Dinner							
Evening							
Night							
Good night							

January	February	March	April	May	June	July	August	September	October	November	December

Figure 5.3 Revealing customer activities and interaction with firm.

The notion of the customer universe is important as it holds the key to understanding how true customer loyalty is generated. If the firm is not present or not competitive in all the competitive arenas of relevance and importance to a given customer type, space is left open for the competition to build relationships. In contrast, if the firm is present in all of these competitive arenas and adapts its behaviors and ways of making decisions to those of the customer, values and beliefs are shared and the foundation for true customer loyalty is present.

The concept of the customer universe also offers a way to understand market dynamics and market creation. Thus, the market dynamics arise due to the way firms are inflicting changes to customer expectations within the competitive arenas. Based on the deep insights into the competitive arenas provided by CUBEical segmentation, firms can achieve market leadership in one or more arenas and thereby fundamentally change the rules of the game.

As demonstrated, roles and scenes are easily identified through facilitated workshops with the customer-facing employees or through customer focus groups and observations. In the next chapter, we will combine all three dimensions of the CUBEical segmentation framework to define and explore the total market of a firm.

6

CUBEical segmentation – the platform for achieving market leadership

THROUGH THE DISCUSSIONS ABOUT CUSTOMER TYPES (Chapter 4) and roles and scenes (Chapter 5), the three dimensions of CUBEical segmentation are developed. In this chapter, we summarize our ideas about good segmentation by discussing the CUBEical segmentation framework from three perspectives:

1. CUBEical segmentation as the platform for defining and gaining insight into markets;

2. CUBEical segmentation as the platform for understanding and driving customer needs and expectations and thereby for outcompeting competitors by setting the market agenda;

3. CUBEical segmentation as the platform for guiding customers effectively through the AIDA process to ensure action, i.e. market share.

To put things into perspective we present a case from the public transportation sector.

CUBEical segmentation in the public transportation sector

In Chapters 4 and 5 we identified the three dimensions spanning the CUBEical segmentation framework: Customer types, roles and scenes (Figure 6.1). We outlined how the CUBEical segmentation framework can be used to structure the tacit customer knowledge held by the customer-facing employees and make this knowledge explicit by employing customer types to describe customer behaviors and ways of making decisions and roles and scenes to describe the situations in which the customers interact with their suppliers.

Let's apply the CUBEical segmentation framework to a public transportation firm. The first step in identifying the CUBEical

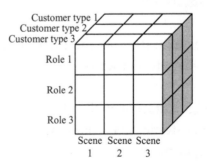

Figure 6.1 CUBEical segmentation framework.

segmentation framework for the public transportation firm is to arrange a number of workshops with customer-facing employees (e.g. bus drivers, train conductors, ticket office personnel) to reveal and describe the various customer types. The outcome of these workshops could be customer type descriptions like the following three:

- Customer type 1 – The Enthusiast: These customers are using public transport all the time. When thinking of transportation, they only think of public transportation. Among the many good reasons for this are environmental considerations combined with the anticipated costs and hassle of owning a car. These customers will enthusiastically support the public transportation firm by promoting the advantages of public transport. They accept service failures as natural, as they accept that this happens with other means of transportation, too.

  What do satisfied Enthusiasts say about the public transportation firm?

  - They offer great service.

  - They are almost always on schedule.

  - Their trains and buses are nice and clean.

- Customer type 2 – The Optimizer: These customers only use public transport when other means of transportation are less optimal. When thinking of transportation, these customers weigh the advantages and disadvantages of different means of transportation – and decide on whatever fits best. When using public transport, these customers are quite happy with the service but the public transportation firm has to be aware that service failures potentially have implications for future decisions as to the attractiveness of their services vis-à-vis other means of transportation.

What do satisfied Optimizers say about the public transportation firm?

- They are really efficient with their booking system.

- Information on departures and prices are excellent.

- Going intercity it is much faster and less expensive than by car.

• Customer type 3 – The Car driver: These customers try to avoid public transport and will only use public transport in an emergency. Thinking of transportation, scheduled departures and masses of other people are the worst nightmare for these customers. When using public transport these customers are angry from the start and point out all the negative sides of public transport. Actually they can be considered non-customers which the public transportation firm sometimes has to serve.

What do satisfied Car drivers say about the public transportation firm?

- As far as public transportation is concerned it is not that bad.

- I can park my car next to the station.

- It is actually quite comfortable but still not as good as sitting in my own car.

Having identified these customer types the next step is to call in the customer-facing employees to identify the competitive arenas, i.e. the roles and scenes in which interaction with customers takes place. As discussed, a customer activities chart like the one shown in Figure 6.2 provides a good overview for the discussions at the workshops. Tickets are booked and paid for, passengers need to get to the point of departure, passengers wait for the service to commence, they are in transit, and then they disembark.

As the customer-facing employees follow the customers through their universes, they identify a number of different scenes, e.g. at home and at work, primarily relevant for planning and booking, and scenes such as on the way to

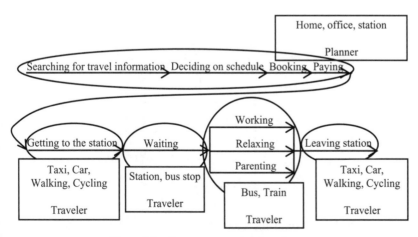

Figure 6.2 Customer activities chart.

and from the station or bus stop, on the platform waiting, and in the train or bus primarily relevant for the journey itself.

The customer-facing employees know that significant differences between customers are observable while traveling, i.e. differences which point out different roles: Some passengers try to concentrate on some paperwork or work with their laptop or read papers. They do not communicate with others – let's call them business travelers. Other passengers chat with the people around them, most likely people they travel together with – let's consider them leisure travelers. And another group of customers is busy looking after their kids (not too close to the platform edge, not too loud and wild, maybe playing a game) – let's call them family travelers. As planning and booking is rather different from traveling, we consider this an extra role – the planner.

The customer-facing employees' insight into the public transport passengers' universes results in the following CUBEical segmentation framework (Figure 6.3).

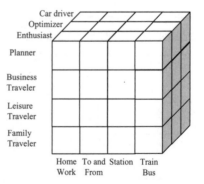

Figure 6.3 CUBEical segmentation for public transportation.

CUBEical segmentation – the platform for defining markets

In Chapter 5 we introduced the notion of the competitive arenas and the notion of the customer universe. We also discussed that competitive arenas vary with regards to importance to the customers belonging to the customer universe in question. Thus, a firm needs to unfold its CUBEical segmentation frameworks to identify those competitive arenas that are very important (marked with a black dot), those where less important interactions with customers take place on a more sporadic basis (marked with a white dot) and those of no relevance where no interaction takes place between the customer and the firm or its peers (no marked). Figure 6.4 illustrates the above mentioned marking.

The CUBEical segmentation framework enables firms to consider the specific market size and market share associated

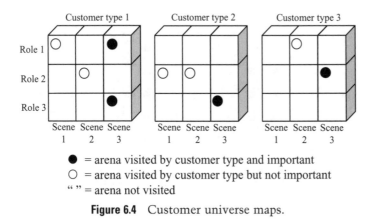

● = arena visited by customer type and important
○ = arena visited by customer type but not important
" " = arena not visited

Figure 6.4   Customer universe maps.

with a specific customer type, i.e. the size of the *market corresponding to the customer universe of a given customer type*. Furthermore, by combining the competitive arenas of the customer types, a firm's *total market* and corresponding total market share can be estimated. Hereby, CUBEical segmentation is breaking new ground in bringing relevance to measuring market size and share.

Returning to the public transportation example, the customer-facing employees can map the competitive arenas of the individual customer types by systematically identifying the combinations of roles and scenes in which interactions take place for each customer type and by allocating importance judgments (Figure 6.5). Here are a few arguments:

- The Enthusiasts do not really plan – they know the schedules better than the public transportation firm's own service personnel! They use a monthly, quarterly

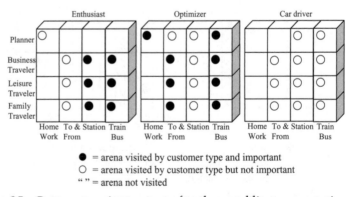

Figure 6.5 Customer universe maps for three public transportation customer types.

or yearly travel pass which gets extended automatically. As they are frequent travelers, the bus or train and the boarding and disembarking facilities are very important for them.

- The Optimizer generally values the opportunity to plan the travel in advance – this is where these customers make their decisions. Not having access to travel information and prices will drive the Optimizers nuts. They usually arrive at the last minute to the train or bus – everything is optimized – thus they do not need platform facilities. Important to them is the experience of traveling by train or bus and efficient, integrated connection to and from the public transport.

- The Car drivers never plan to use public transport – they try to avoid it! For them, nothing but the car works. The whole experience to them is not good – they try to survive their time in public transport and hope that it will be a long time until they have to go by bus or train again.

Based on this mapping the public transportation firm has obtained a clear picture of the *customer universes* of their three customer types. An individual customer experiences the universe according to their customer type. The transportation firm, in addition to the market size and market share for each of the customer universes in question, of course, also gets a picture of the *total market* by combining the three universes. All interactions between the firm and its competitors on one side and the customers on the other are included in the identified cubes.

CUBEical segmentation – the platform for revealing customer needs and setting customer expectations

The stability of customer types, roles and scenes does not conflict with markets being highly dynamic. Yet the important point to remember is that it is not customers who are moving targets, it is their expectations. Customer expectations are subject to change due to changes in technology (technological dynamics) and due to competition (competitive dynamics). In most cases, changes in customer expectations are inflicted by firms themselves – firms create dynamics within the universes, not of the universes.

No matter the size and scope of the firm, whether global, regional or local, or high-tech or low-tech, everybody agrees that customer needs and customer expectations must be in focus. The logic of the statement is convincingly strong as it holds the *raison d'être* of all firms: Firms exist to serve their customers by fulfilling customers' needs and expectations – consistently failing to do so results in going out of business.

Despite being the foundation pillars for business, needs and expectations are subject to a high degree of ambiguity – similar to the ambiguity of situations and occasions. Needs are often described at too high levels to be of business value. How do needs like "thirst" or "self-expression" translate into specific product development initiatives? On the other hand, needs are seldom distinguished from the dynamic part, namely the change in customers' expectations inflicted by the firms themselves. As such, needs and expectations are often used interchangeably in business.

But there is an important difference between needs and expectations. Customer expectations are the views of a customer on how a firm should address the customer needs. Thus, the expectation is about the solution; the need is about the challenge to be solved. The expectation is about how the firm does a job for the customer; the need is the job itself. Thus, the need is the outcome the customer wants to achieve; the expectation is the way this outcome is achieved. Needs are stable, expectations are dynamic and, as mentioned, typically inflicted by the firms themselves.

Take, for example, a business traveler whose needs could be safe, on schedule, comfortable transportation and good communication lines back to headquarters. Have these needs changed since the time of Marco Polo? Probably not! What about customers´ expectations? Definitely! Today, good communication means that the customers expect high speed internet connections and hot-spots along the route. At the time of Marco Polo, the customer expected that things were arranged so that homebound and outbound camel caravans regularly met along the route. What have changed are not customer needs but customer expectations.

The CUBEical segmentation framework is breaking new ground in providing firms with a framework for exploring needs at the competitive arena level. Based on this insight into the competitive arenas, firms are enabled to search proactively for opportunities for setting customer expectations beyond the reach of competition. Herewith, a firm is enabled to execute market creation, understood as the creation of new expectations and subsequent delivery. Firms exist not only to serve the present expectations of their customers. If they want to prosper they must also drive their markets, i.e. addressing customer needs in innovative ways and, thus, setting new expectations and challenging their competitors. Alternatively, firms may seek to address customer needs currently not served at all – the black holes of the customer universe. For that matter, the distinction between needs and expectations is of paramount importance. Only working with customer expectations as expressed by customers – a common problem of customer-led innovation processes – limits the scope for radical innovation.

There are three opportunities for driving markets:

1. Opportunities in competitive arenas already being served by the firm – by introducing new goods or services;

2. Opportunities in entering competitive arenas currently not served by the firm but served by competitors – by introducing new competitive goods or services;

3. Opportunities in entering new competitive arenas, thus extending the activated part of the customer universe of the customer type in question.

CUBEical segmentation provides a framework for systematically identifying market opportunities and for assessing the market potential for driving profitable revenue growth. This represents a radical shift towards execution based on deep customer insights as opposed to being blindfolded when trying to pin down customer needs. Thus, as long as customer behavior is unexplainable, addressing customer needs and expectations in communication and product management is a mission impossible.

Without an upfront understanding of customer needs and customer expectations, customer satisfaction reviews keep followers trapped in a dead-end street with their fellow followers. Customer needs and expectations cannot be revealed from customer satisfaction studies. The follower can only respond reactively to what their surveys reveal and consequently they will stay followers. The market is experienced as a black box and customers as moving targets. These shortcomings of current business practice are overcome with CUBEical segmentation (Figure 6.6).

Mapping of the competitive arenas provides a powerful platform for identifying, accessing, prioritizing and selecting opportunities for competitive actions:

- The competitive arenas and an indication of the importance of the arenas seen through the eyes of the customer type in question are mapped. Hereby, the target arenas for building true customer loyalty are highlighted.

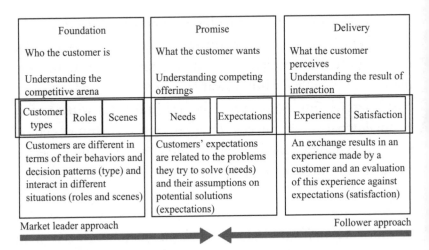

Figure 6.6 Revealing customer needs and setting expectations.

- In addition, the firm can discuss which of the inactive arenas has the potential to attract customers.

We continue this discussion in Chapter 7 where the process of transforming the customer and market universe maps into a firm strategy is described in detail.

CUBEical segmentation – the platform for customer management through the AIDA process

When introducing the idea of making the customer the pivotal focus on the executive agenda for driving profitable revenue growth, we concluded that inadequate customer segmentation had blocked the road for implementing this agenda. Without a common language for harvesting, structuring, sharing and leveraging upon the customer knowledge of the firm, not only the executives struggle, but also marketing and sales have severe difficulties in working together on managing customers throughout the AIDA process (Figure 6.7). The efforts for gaining customer insight through applying CUBEical segmentation prove their worth by guiding customers effectively and successfully through the AIDA process, thus enabling profitable revenue growth.

The customer insight provided by the CUBEical segmentation framework is hereby addressing one of today's major challenges for sales and marketing, namely communications. Many communications end in wasting resources because firms and customers talk at each other, not with each other. One fundamental problem of marketing and sales is the dominance of product selling: A presentation of the many features of products aims at impressing customers but actually bores and confuses them because the features probably

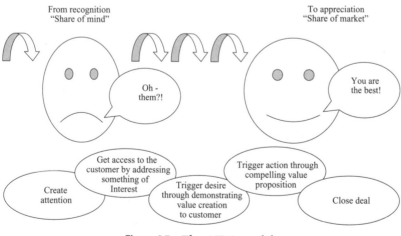

Figure 6.7 The AIDA model.

are not relevant to the customer. Customer communication can only succeed when the customer receives information that fits to the things he has in mind – if only we knew what is on the minds of our customers.

The insight from customer types, roles and scenes defines the needs and expectations of customers and, thus, structures what is on their minds. This knowledge is valid not only for identifying opportunities for profitable revenue growth and market leadership but also for acting on these opportunities.

The AIDA process of catching a customer's *Attention* through targeted communication or branding will only succeed when the message has a relevant content, i.e. addresses a need and sets relevant expectations. In addition, the way of communicating must be adapted to the customer universe: In which role and in which scene can and should a firm address the customer? CUBEical segmentation offers the necessary insight to design effective communication content and means.

Branding is, in a nutshell, the systematic uploading of values and beliefs so that customers can download and relate these values and beliefs to their own (Figure 6.8). Logically, an understanding of customer values and beliefs is necessary to design effective branding strategies and campaigns. Therewith, it is impossible to brand towards demo-firmo-graphic segments – branding is what a firm can produce in the customer's mind. As such, insight into the mind of customers is what makes branding successful. Here, the CUBEical segmentation framework provides the required insight.

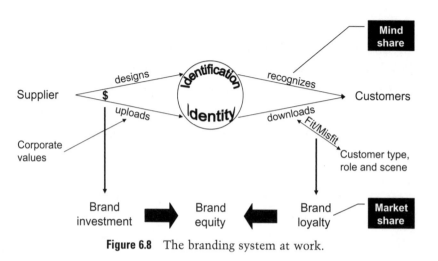

Figure 6.8   The branding system at work.

To move a customer forward in the AIDA model and to raise the *Interest* of the customer, the firm must address the specific needs of customers through its offerings and communication. The insight into competitive arenas is a prerequisite for creating interest. Actually, communication should be oriented towards the interest stage. Purely awareness-oriented campaigns are rather meaningless because they require yet another costly campaign to move customers further in the AIDA process. Interestingly, a lot of communication today is awareness focused. Think of the many TV spots and print media advertisements that pass through your own universe: You probably cannot even remember the firm yet alone the message. This is a clear sign of untargeted communication which does not address a relevant need. As such, customers might have a short-term awareness but no interest. Such ineffective communication is not worth its money.

When trying to trigger the customer's *Desire* for the goods or services offered or when trying to trigger the customer to take

Action and close the deal, a firm needs to base its efforts on an understanding of customer needs. While awareness and interest can happen by accident, desire and action depend on customers seeing the offering of a firm as a valuable solution to a need, i.e. customers have a positive expectation to what the firm can do for them. Otherwise, customers will never desire nor pay for the goods and services.

Yes, this logic is trivial. But the frightening truth is that still many communication efforts never hit a target. CUBE-ical segmentation provides a strong platform for closing deals effectively. Winning business is about managing customers through the AIDA process – through the whole process. Only a closed deal (action) provides market share, profitable revenue growth, return on investment – or whatever one may wish to call it. We explain implementation in more detail in Chapter 8.

The end of the discovery – towards action

We started our tour by looking at the executive agenda and discovered four important aspects: One, executives want to achieve profitable revenue growth – they have EBITDA on their mind. Two, the only way to achieve EBITDA growth is to look at customers and increase market efficiency. Three, whatever marketing and sales does, it must adhere to the executive requirements of context, accountability and results. Four, the underlying problem for not achieving market efficiency is bad segmentation practice.

We then turned to current segmentation practice and discovered three criteria of good segmentation practice:

- Customer segments must be intuitively recognizable: If not, the executives and customer-facing employees cannot differentiate between customers and a business strategy based on differentiation among customers will fail in its development and in its implementation. Segmentation must capture the real context of a customer in order to be understandable and manageable.

- Customer segments must be stable with regard to segment membership: If not, customers will be in one segment at one time and in another segment at another time. Which differentiation strategy should then apply? Furthermore, if segment membership is not stable the segmentation cannot support knowledge sharing and leveraging the organization's joint customer knowledge.

- Customer segments must be effective in the market by reflecting the needs and expectations of the customers: If not, actions taken by the firm based on the segmentation make no sense to customers and thus implementation of the firm's strategy has no impact on revenues.

While searching for a segmentation framework satisfying the three criteria, we discovered three dimensions: Customer types, roles and scenes. With this CUBEical segmentation framework, we developed a better understanding of markets, argued for its usability for identifying opportunities and pictured its usefulness for driving the AIDA process.

As such, the discovery is over. What is left is hard work – firms need to activate the customer universe, they need to live it. By now, we know the customer universe. In order to come from customer universe (CU) to Customer Universe Based Execution (CUBE), we need to turn our attention to execution. There are two elements to this: Developing a strategy for the market universe and implementing the strategy into effective marketing and sales programs. This is what we call Part II of the tour: Activating the customer universe.

PART II

Activating the customer universe

Having discovered the customer universes it is time to activate the universes by leveraging on the customer insight gained. This activation has two parts: Strategy, i.e. making a plan, and implementation, i.e. making the plan work.

For activating the executive agenda of profitable revenue growth, we first demonstrate how the customer universe forms the foundation for developing customer strategies. This is a three-step process which transforms the universe maps into strategy maps. Strategy is about where and how to compete. The notion of competitive arenas makes these strategies very detailed and yet highly operational and intuitively understandable.

Having a strategy is good, activating the strategy throughout the firm is better. Thus, the next step is implementation. Keeping the focus on profitable revenue growth in mind we discuss up- and cross-sales. Also, we discuss branding and customer communications, the means of addressing the attention and interest of the customers.

7

CUBEical strategy – where and how to compete

A S DISCUSSED IN THE PREVIOUS CHAPTERS, CUBEICAL segmentation lives up to good segmentation practice and executive requirements. By applying CUBEical segmentation customers are made the pivotal focus on the executive agenda of driving profitable revenue growth. The remaining question is: How? Now that we know the dimensions of the customer universe and thereby are enabled to reveal customer needs and expectations, the challenge is to position the firm within the customer universe by deciding upon where and how to compete in order to gain market leadership.

Firms want to build firm-specific customer strategies – nothing else is useful for executives and managers. And firms need to build firm-specific customer strategies because any strategy must not only be customer focused, but also honor the firm's specific history and its current enablers and barriers for future actions. A strategy is the way to achieve a firm's targets; some may wish to say fulfill its mission or its vision. As the strategy is regarding the way from today's position of the firm to a position in the future, today's position is important for defining the starting point. Defining the starting point also enables the firm to judge if the future position is realistic and, thus, a motivating target for the employees. Realistic does not imply "no ambition" or "do what you have always done"; it means feasible beyond the obvious.

We therefore start our strategy discussion by explaining a firm's universe – the universe coexisting alongside the market universe. Based on this understanding, we will present our way of turning the customer and market universe maps into customer and market strategy maps.

The firm universe

So far we have been focusing on customers for gaining insight into customer needs and expectations. In order to build valid and valuable strategies, a good understanding of the firm is also important. Our understanding of the firm universe is illustrated in Figure 7.1.

From a strategy point of view, the challenge of the firm is to find the formula for combining all of its strategic options to address customer needs and preferably to set customer expectations beyond the reach of the competition. As illustrated, customer expectations are driven by firm offerings. Offerings in turn are driven by competences and competences by types, roles and scenes. Therefore, the options related to strategic decision-making are found in firm type, roles, scenes,

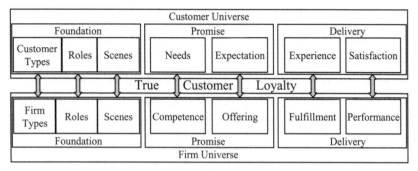

Figure 7.1 CUBEical relationship framework.

competencies and offerings. These elements combined form the strategy, while fulfillment and performance are reflecting the implementation of the strategy: Has the firm succeeded in its strategy? If fulfillment fails to match the strategy, the firm will miss its performance targets as customer expectations are not fulfilled and customer satisfaction levels consequently are low.

Regarding the foundation of customer relationships, firms, just like customers, are described through the three stable intuitively recognizable dimensions: types, roles and scenes.

Firm type, i.e. the behavior and decision-making patterns of a firm vis-à-vis a given customer type, is experienced by a customer through the interactions taking place and the firm's offerings within the competitive arenas. One challenge for a firm is the adaptation of the firm's behaviors and decision-making patterns vis-à-vis the identified customer types. The notion of firm types is the core of the strategic options linked to differentiation. According to their customer differentiation strategies, firms behave differently towards different groups of customers, identified as different customer types. For example, Microsoft is perceived differently by an original equipment manufacturer (OEM) as opposed to a local one-man IT support firm. Obviously, for a good working relationship between the firm and a given customer type, the customer-experienced firm type and the customer type need to match each other. Only this match ensures that the relationship will work.

Similar to customers, a firm's behaviors and ways of making decisions are based on the firm's values and beliefs. These values and beliefs are typically made explicit through corporate culture statements and programs. In addition to driving external communications, such programs are aimed at aligning the behaviors and decisions of the employees to the firm's customer strategies and to its overall market strategy, i.e. to guide the employees' behaviors and decision-making patterns to match the different customer types being served. This implies that the firm's corporate values and beliefs must span the varying behaviors and decision-making patterns of the individual customer types. Thus, firms either have broad corporate values and beliefs to enable serving various customer types or have narrowly defined corporate values making the firm a niche operator for a limited set of customer types. The challenge of the broader values is to avoid being trapped in the middle and thus undifferentiated and not attractive to the customers. The challenge of the narrow values is growth as the firm is limited to its designated customer types.

In this context, corporate values and beliefs are stable. Assuming that the firm is pursuing long lasting relationships and that there are no outside factors forcing the firm to change its overall strategy or resource allocation across customer types radically (e.g. mergers and acquisitions), the firm type as seen through the eyes of the individual customer types is stable, mirroring the stability of customer types.

Thus, firm types are among the parameters which a firm can model while laying its strategy. Actually, when a firm decides upon which competitive arenas to address and how to address them, this influences the firm's behaviors and ways of decision-making *as experienced by the customer*. Hereby, within the boundaries of corporate values and beliefs, firm type is modeled through strategy.

Roles and scenes are also among the strategic options which the firm employs in developing its strategy. Thus, it can decide to address or not to address customers in a given role or in a given scene. A firm can decide to pull in or out of a competitive arena.

In developing a strategy, a firm must take into account that the roles it plays must match the roles of the customer. Within the competitive arena, the firm must play a role compatible with the customer's role. Just like in the theater: Juliet needs a Romeo to perform. This is the only way a meaningful interaction can take place. If the firm does not play its role correctly, the customer will not realize the supplier as "being there" – and, thus, no interaction takes place and the competitive arena is lost.

The same argument applies to scenes. While roles must be compatible, scenes must be the same. Again, if not on the scene, no interaction takes place and the competitive arena is lost. This applies physically: If a firm sells in Europe and the customers are buying in the US, no business is conducted. And electronically: When customers look for information on the internet and a firm does not provide relevant information there, the competitive arena is lost.

In the CUBEical relationship framework, types, roles and scenes are building the foundation for any business interaction to take place. Incompatible ways of behavior and decision-making, incompatible roles and different scenes prevent firms from interacting with customers. Missing out on these points, no manager has to be concerned about the rest of the model – it is simply not relevant. Understanding the three dimensions, the following issues can be addressed.

Firm types, roles and scenes determine the required competencies for being competitive. With this link, the CUBEical framework offers an assessment tool for what a firm needs and what it does not need for competing in the chosen arenas. Competencies are combinations of resources, skills and knowledge which enable the production of an outcome. For long-term customer relationships, a firm's competencies and a firm's ambitions to develop its competencies in the future must match customer needs and customer expectations. Therefore, the use and development of the firm's competencies are among the very important strategic options facing the firm when developing a strategy.

The outcome of production is presented to customers during the sales process as an offering. The offering is what the firm has decided and is able to do. It is the major force in setting customer expectations and thus an important element in developing the strategy. In contrast to customers' prior experience, competitive offerings, third party information and projections of the future, the offering is the most controllable element of setting expectations as it is in the hands of the firm itself.

As illustrated in Figure 7.1, competencies and offerings are regarded as the promise of the firm. The promises are laid out in the strategy and designed to match the different needs and expectations of the individual customer types. The offering is today's offering; competencies are the basis for tomorrow's offerings. As more and more customers are interested in long-term relationships, they assess a firm's competencies to ensure themselves that choosing a certain supplier is the right decision for today and for tomorrow. As such, competencies are also on offer – even though a firm will not sell its competencies as such to customers. Selling competencies is called mergers and acquisitions.

The third part of the framework is delivery. Once chosen, firms fulfill their obligations, striving to live up to the cutomer expectations set by the firm. Well, at least they try. Reality shows that fulfillment does not always live up to offerings. Production breakdown, shortage of material, traffic jams and, worst of all, overselling contribute to a different fulfillment than promised. Customers experience fulfillment and any customer experience will be measured against the promise the firm made. Like a pop song once pronounced:

"Remember the promise you made". Based on experiences and expectations, customers are either satisfied or not.

Failure to fulfill will also show up in the performance measures of the firm indicating to what extent the firm has been successful in implementing its strategy. Performance is measured in many dimensions these days: EBITDA, revenue, customer satisfaction ratings, waiting time statistics, failure rates, just to mention a few. These measures indicate to the firm if and where corrective actions have to be taken to keep strategy implementation on track, or where strategy has to be corrected to mirror reality.

With this explanation of the framework, the strategy discussion can begin. Figure 7.2 illustrates the roadmap for developing a CUBEical strategy. The first step – namely, creating the foundation for the strategy by establishing a good segmentation framework – is already behind us: Chapter 4 showed the way to customer types, Chapter 5 guided us through the universe in terms of roles and scenes, and Chapter 6 brought the segmentation dimensions together and introduced the notion of varying importance of competitive arenas. Let's enter the second step: Let's turn the universe map into a competition map.

Turning the universe map into the competition map

By completing CUBEical segmentation, the firm has mapped out the customers' universes for each of the customer

	Specific customer type level: **CUSTOMER**	All customer types level: **MARKET**
Foundation Identification of customer types, roles and scenes	customer type + roles and scenes + customer arena importance = CUSTOMER *UNIVERSE* MAPS	customer types + roles and scenes + customer arena importance = MARKET *UNIVERSE* MAP
Delivery Identification of current customer(s) experience across competitors and with the firm	customer satisfaction + competitor and firm positions + firm fulfillment = CUSTOMER *COMPETITION* MAPS (as is)	customer satisfaction + competitor and firm position + firm fulfillment = MARKET *COMPETITION* MAP (as is)
Promise Identification of new opportunities in currently active and inactive arenas (innovation and market creation)	new expectations in old arenas + new needs in new arenas + feasibility check = CUSTOMER *OPPORTUNITY* MAPS (could be)	new expectations in old arenas + new needs in new arenas + feasibility check = MARKET *OPPORTUNITY* MAP (could be)
ROI Identification of business impact and investments per arena and prioritization of investments across arenas per customer type and for whole market	arena business impact + required arena investments + prioritization of arenas	arena business impact + required arena investments + prioritization of arenas
Result Optimal resource allocation regarding market and resource efficiency, thus profitable revenue growth road map (EBITDA growth)	= CUSTOMER *STRATEGY* MAPS (to be)	= MARKET *STRATEGY* MAP (to be)

Figure 7.2 Development steps for CUBEical strategy – from universe map to strategy map.

types, including the identification of the importance of the competitive arenas to the customers. Based on this insight, firms need to expand their understanding of the as-is competitive situation within the individual customer universes and therewith within the overall market universe. This extended understanding of competition has three dimensions:

1. How satisfied are customers with the way their needs and expectations are addressed by the suppliers, i.e. the firm and its competitors?

2. In which competitive arenas does the firm compete?

3. What is the firm's position relative to its competitors within the arenas in which the firm competes, i.e. is the firm a market leader or a follower?

Re 1: Satisfying customer needs

First, the overall customer satisfaction with the current offerings in each competitive arena is analyzed. In contrast to firm-specific satisfaction studies, the focus here is on market satisfaction across competitors: How satisfied are customers with current offerings regardless of the supplier? Based on the customer universe map the firm can literally enter each competitive arena and assess customer needs through the eyes of the customer. These needs are the reference points when measuring customer satisfaction vis-à-vis competition within and across the arenas. For simplicity reasons, three levels are used to rank customer satisfaction in Figure 7.3:

- Customers are very satisfied with the current offerings in the market (indicated with a happy face); i.e. customers' needs are fully fulfilled;

- Customers are neither satisfied nor dissatisfied with the current offerings in the market, i.e. they could wish their needs somewhat better fulfilled but overall they are happy with the offerings (indicated with a neutral face);

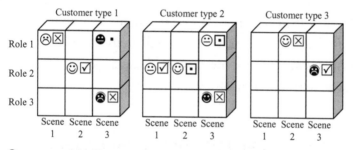

● = arena visited by customer type and important
○ = arena visited by customer type but not important
" " = arena not visited

☺ = customers satisfied with current market experience
☻ = customers partially dissatisfied with current market experience
☹ = customers dissatisfied
" " = no customer present

☑ = firm offering market leader in arena
⊡ = firm offering keeps up with competition
☒ = firm offering lacks behind competition
▪ = firm not present but competitors are
" " = no supplier present

Figure 7.3   The competition maps.

- Customers are dissatisfied as their needs are not fulfilled resulting in customers actively searching for new solutions and/or complaining to the firms about the deliveries (indicated with an unhappy face).

Re 2: Firm and competitor positions across the customer universes

As we already pointed out, firms typically do not address all competitive arenas. This differentiation can be based on the CUBEical dimensions: Customer types (some jewelers only address highly individual, special design-interested customers), roles (the Italian sports car manufacturer Lamborghini has no family cars), or scenes (Dell does not offer its PCs in shops). As such, an overview of the players per competitive arena reveals their strategy focus.

Re 3: Firm's competitive position within competitive arenas

To complete the competition maps, the firm's competitive position within those arenas where it competes are assessed using the square with a tick mark to indicate that the firm is market leader, a square with a dot to indicate that the firm is a follower keeping up with its peers and a square with an X to indicate that the firm is lagging behind competition.

The as-is competitive situation is described by mapping out the above dimensions on the customer universe maps and on the market universe map. Therewith, the universe maps turn into customer competition maps and the market competition map as outlined in Figure 7.3.

Figure 7.3 illustrates a complete, firm-specific picture of the customer universes in relation to the firm and its competitive position.

The competition maps indicate customers' satisfaction with current experiences, i.e. how well the suppliers in total fulfill customer needs and expectations. Likewise, the firm's rating against competitors indicates the competitiveness of the firm's competencies, offerings and fulfillment. Overall, the competition maps are simple charts providing major insights.

Turning the competition map into the opportunity map

Having outlined the competitive as-is universes, it is time to look for future opportunities, i.e. to identify the firm's future potential promises to customers, and to map these on the opportunity map. When identifying future opportunities the firm must systematically go through the competitive arenas and challenge the status quo as given in the competition maps. The challenge for all competitive arenas is to identify new ways of setting customer expectations beyond the reach of competition. This challenge can be handled systematically based on the developed understanding of the customer universes: Knowing customer type, role and scene offers a deep insight into customer needs. This in turn creates a deep understanding of how future customer expectations can be proactively set based on the firm's knowledge about the situation in which customer needs unfold. This makes the competition maps ideal platforms for stimulating the creativity of the firm.

The different combinations of symbols also offer some more specific subquestions (Figure 7.4) – because the main question remains as above: How can the firm set customer expectations beyond the reach of its competitors?

In terms of finding concrete ideas for opportunities, there is free choice of all creativity methods and market research methods; observations, decision trees, thinking hats, anthropology – you name it. The important difference between normal use of these methods and use in connection with developing a CUBEical strategy is the specific definition of competitive arenas. While all other approaches leave these techniques to randomly search for customer needs across the universes (by not knowing competitive arenas), firms are now in a position to look for creative solutions to specifically known customer needs within a given arena.

While using the eyes of a customer type, the firm must enter all arenas, no matter whether they are served by the firm or not, and try to identify new ways of setting customer expectations beyond the reach of competition by introducing new offerings and, thus, improving fulfillment. The question to ask is: Given that I behave and decide the way I do (customer

Firm Customer	" "	•	☒	⊡	☑
☺	How can we set an agenda by addressing the needs of these customers? As a minimum, how can we match our competitors?				How can we keep our lead and improve our offering?
☺					
☹					
" "	How can we set an agenda in this unpopulated arena and get customers to join?	How can we improve our performance to match or even outperform our competitors in order to get customers to join?			How can we keep our lead until customers arrive? How can we get customers?

Figure 7.4 Different competitive constellations and key questions.

type) in this situation (role and scene), as to the problems I have to get solved (needs), what could my supplier offer (expectation) and do (experience) to solve my problems even better than today (satisfaction)?

The competition map fuels efficient discussion of new ideas. With the competitive maps at hand, any idea from R&D can be discussed as to where it fits: The solution you are envisioning, for which arena is it suitable? This increases the level of discussion and the level of acceptance of idea rejection. And it increases – over time – the understanding of customers by non-customer-facing employees. Because the universes with their three dimensions – customer types, roles and scenes – are intuitively understandable and stable, non-customer-facing employees like R&D and accounting people swiftly get the picture and start thinking from inside the customers' universes.

Opportunities for future actions of a firm are not only to make things better, higher, faster, bigger. It could just as well be about scaling down or leaving an arena. Scaling down has two forms.

One scenario is a corrective action to "overshooting" the target, taking features out of the offering which do not create value for the customer, i.e. these features do not address a customer need, nor are they expected. In recent years, software has been supplied without handbooks and installation manuals. For those few needing manuals, they are now directed to the web. Thus, the majority of customers do not feel a drop in value, they actually appreciate the saving on disposal costs. In this case, the firm can achieve higher resource efficiency at stable market efficiency.

The other scenario is where the firm strategically decides to give an arena lower priority and reduce resource investments knowing that customer satisfaction will decrease. This scenario represents the classical trade-off between resource efficiency and market efficiency. The latter case is not directly supporting market leadership opportunities; it is merely an option to finance it by freeing up resources to be allocated to other more important arenas. This issue is dealt with in the next section.

For the opportunity map, we also need to signal all those arenas where we can gain market leadership by reducing our current offering. Typical arenas are those where the firm has a leading position which can be maintained by even less resource allocation or those where the firm invests but no customers have arrived yet.

While the creative process can produce all sorts of ideas, an opportunity map is only valid when populated with realistic and feasible ideas. A firm has to evaluate the feasibility of setting customer expectations and delivering on these by taking into account its current and future competencies, its offerings and its overall resources. The feasibility of opportunities implies that the firm is able to deliver on the idea but also that the offering envisioned is potentially attractive to the customers.

In addition, this step identifies opportunities which are not in the strategic scope of the firm given its corporate values and corporate strategies. Consider the following case: A wood processing firm aims at positioning itself as a top quality supplier. The firm can, of course, manufacture lower quality products and there are plenty of opportunities to do so. But it would ruin the firm's strategy because personnel and machines would not be prepared to take up the higher end production. Too much of the firm's capital is tied up in machines which do not fit the strategy of the firm. Too many firms invest in opportunities which, seen in isolation, are good business cases but which in relation to the corporate goals only steal focus and finance from the important part of the business. If opportunities do not fit the corporate agenda, their realization will not fit either.

These three requirements of feasibility – technically possible for the firm, attractive to the customer and compatible with the firm's corporate values and strategies – should not be seen rigidly. Such interpretation hinders radical innovation. But populating the opportunity matrix with ideas which by no means make sense is not helpful either. An opportunity is something which can be achieved; anything else is a fiction.

Again, the competition map offers the basis for a well-informed and systematic discussion of opportunities and their feasibility. In the customer opportunity maps and the corresponding market opportunity map, opportunities are marked with stars on their respective competitive arenas. These maps provide great business value for strategic planning because they provide the firm with an intuitive, easy-to-understand and coherent description of business opportunities spanning from the individual competitive arenas, over the customer universes to the firm's total market. Based on the firm's insights into the needs of the customers as seen through the customers' eyes the opportunity maps reveal where and how the firm potentially could set customer expectations beyond the reach of competition (Figure 7.5).

Turning the opportunity map into the strategy map

Regarding where and how to compete, CUBEical strategy is about prioritizing the scarce resources of the firm vis-à-vis the

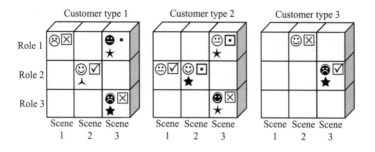

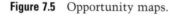

★ = opportunity for setting expectations (leading competition)
⭐ = opportunity for matching expectations (following competition)
⅄ = opportunity for reducing investments (leaving competition)
" " = no opportunity – keep status quo

Figure 7.5 Opportunity maps.

opportunities for driving profitable revenue growth as identified in the opportunity maps. In most firms, the opportunity map offers too many opportunities with regard to the firm's resources. Therefore, prioritization of opportunities is required within and across the customer universes in order to identify the combination of opportunities which together with the unchanged presence in some arenas maximize the return on investments given the overall resource constraints. A firm's customer strategy maps and market strategy map specify how the firm will drive its business across customer types. The transformation from opportunities into strategy is a two step process:

A: Assessing opportunities and unchanged current arenas;

B: Prioritizing opportunities and unchanged current arenas.

Re A: Assessing opportunities and unchanged current arenas

The customer opportunity maps highlight all those opportunities for change which are feasible for each customer type and across customer types. The purpose of the assessment is to assign an ROI rating to each opportunity and to the arenas being left unchanged as the ROI is one selection criterion for prioritizing opportunities and current unchanged arenas in step B. The assessment is made along the following two criteria:

1. Return of opportunity/arena;

2. Investment requirements of opportunity/arena.

Return of opportunity/arena

Compared to a situation where markets and competition seem hard to pin down and where customer needs and expectations are vaguely defined, competitive arenas represent a well-defined structure of the competitive environments and, thus, a sound foundation for evaluating the expected returns from an opportunity. Returns are assessed by considering the importance of the arena to the customer and to the firm interacting with the customer. There are typically three ways returns of opportunities and currently served unchanged arenas are estimated:

•   The opportunity or current presence is within a competitive arena which can be considered a submarket where transactions and consumption take place. For example, friends (role) seeing each other (activity) at the cinema (scene) buy and drink Coke. The assessment will include measures for revenues, profits and not yet harvested market potentials.

- Opportunities or current presence in areas important for the customer have a potentially high return for the firm because not being in the arena means losing the customer in other arenas too. Thus, the importance of being in a specific arena is not measured by the returns from the arena itself but from the consolidated returns across competitive arenas in the customer universe.

- The opportunity or current presence within the arena is related to a decisive situation or occasion in the AIDA process. Creating desire by presenting an offering to the customer's production manager (role) at the customer's production facilities (scene) implies that the customer buys the offering. As such, the competitive arena may not be important to the customer but the arena is important for the firm to make sales.

The assessment will typically be made by considering the effect of executing the opportunity against staying in the arena unchanged: How much business will the firm win when realizing the opportunity against continuing business as usual within an arena?

Competitive arenas are connected to each other not only by customer type but also by a degree of substitution. Another arena can serve as a substitution but not as a replacement.

The production manager above could instead be presented with the offering at a meeting or at a trade fair. To some degree inconvenience is imposed on customers asking them to change role and scene in order to obtain access to a firm's offerings. If customers accept this, brand loyalty or brand strength is used as an explanation. The story of a thirsty person in the desert finally finding a pub but leaving the pub without drinking due to a lack of Coke is an example. Basically, the customer changes scene by trying to get to the next pub. Thus, not realizing an opportunity is seldom a total loss of customers. The estimation is about the degree of gains and losses of business.

Investment requirements of opportunities/arena

Market leadership does not come free of charge. The realization of an opportunity comes at a cost; it is an investment. Likewise, there will typically be investments associated with continuing business the same way as before within an arena. Estimating the level of investments for addressing an opportunity or a competitive arena in general is not always an easy task but still a task which firms usually are quite well prepared to handle. Looking at the individual competitive arenas, the investment is sometimes directly linked to one arena. In these cases, the required investments can be calculated directly. In other instances, the same investment appears across various customer types, roles or scenes. Thus, the investments across various arenas need to be aggregated, not just added. A typical example is the opportunity to invest in a call center or a website for better handling of customer interaction. This investment normally cuts across customer types, roles and scenes as many customers in different roles and scenes are potential users. As such, a more complex solution may be needed so that the investment might be higher than for a single customer type but significantly lower than the sum of individual investments.

Based on the estimation of returns and investments, an ROI can now be assigned to each opportunity and to each of the current arenas not being influenced by the opportunities identified.

Re B: Prioritizing opportunities and unchanged current arenas

To establish the customer strategy maps and market strategy map of the firm, the decision of either realizing an opportunity or not, or the decision to stay in or leave a currently served arena needs to be made. These decisions are made with respect to the resources available, i.e. the sum of chosen opportunities plus today's status quo provides the customer strategies and the market strategy. The aim of prioritizing opportunities is to maximize the accumulated market efficiency vis-à-vis the individual customer types, while at the same time maximizing resource efficiency within and across customer types. This iterative process maximizes the increase in EBITDA possible with the given resources.

When developing the customer strategy maps and the market strategy map, opportunities and unchanged arenas are picked based on the following two criteria:

- ROI (as assigned in step A);

- Fit to business system.

There is no mathematical process for this part. It is more a jigsaw puzzle which is pieced together by trying different constellations. The typical procedure is to pick the opportunity/arena offering the highest ROI. The required investments have to be checked against the available resources. If sufficient resources are available, the impact of realizing the opportunity/arena on the firm's business set-up is evaluated because the implementation of opportunities has to fit the firm's business set-up (Figure 7.5). If the different elements of the business set-up are not aligned, execution becomes impossible. A firm's business set-up has four building blocks:

- CRM set-up: The competencies and offerings required to interact with the customer;

- Channel set-up: The competencies and offerings required by channel partners to serve the customer types;

- Production set-up: The competencies and offerings required in production to serve the customer;

- Supply chain set-up: The competencies and offerings required to drive suppliers.

Hereby, the CRM and channel are substitutes – likewise production and supply chain: All those competencies and offerings not internally provided must be part of the external side. In line with the considerations to maximize ROI it should also be taken into consideration if it makes sense to involve third parties to supplement parts of the business system.

Even when an opportunity or an arena has a high ROI, if it does not fit into the firm's business set-up it cannot be implemented. Typical examples are: Working with retailers, FMCG firms only have limited space in supermarkets. While launching 10 new products across customer types might make sense, the lack of shelf space may limit new products to five per year. Or when customers across customer types demand exclusivity rights, a firm cannot implement various opportunities targeting similar products. Internally, the firm's R&D department may not be able to execute more than three new projects. Thus, there are various constraints which only become visible when placing an opportunity into operation (Figure 7.6).

Along the process, it is constantly considered if ROI can be further increased by consolidating and modifying opportunities and arena investments within or across customer types in order to increase resource efficiency but with a slight decrease in market efficiency. As long as resources are still available, the above process is continued by picking the next opportunity.

It is up to executives to make the final decision on where and how to compete, i.e. to make up the final customer strategy

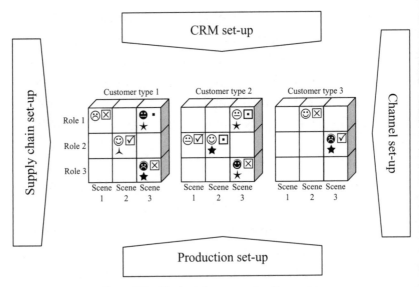

Figure 7.6 Optimizing opportunity maps.

maps and the overall market strategy of the firm. Deciding on the final customer strategy maps is a game without rules influenced by management's ambitions, degree of entrepreneurship and willingness to take risks. There is always a fine line between strategy and tragedy. But with the CUBEical strategy process, the borderline has shifted towards safer ground due to the systematic approach and level of detail provided by the CUBEical maps to which subsequently relevant data was added.

Since establishing the customer universe map, all information collected and decisions made have been registered at competitive arena level and carried on to the next level of competition and opportunity maps. Therefore, there is full traceability and transparency in all the decisions made to complete the overall customer and market strategy maps of the firm. Consequently, compared to traditional ways of working with strategic planning the CUBEical strategy is based on facts, sound judgments, and structure as opposed to wild guessing and unstructured wishful thinking.

In the customer strategy maps and in the overall market strategy map of the firm, the future strategy is documented (Figure 7.7). Due to the intuitive, easy-to-recognize nature of customer type, role and scene framing a competitive arena, the firm is able to walk into the situation as seen through the eyes of the customer. Consequently, the description of the arena strategies can be detailed to a level where the contributions of all functional areas involved in implementing the strategy can be outlined. As a result, business processes can be aligned to provide seamless integration between the firm and the customers. The fundamental weaknesses of functional strategies not being aligned is wiped out by applying the CUBEical strategy framework. Customer strategy maps and the market strategy map provide the firm

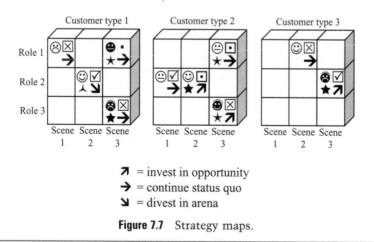

Figure 7.7 Strategy maps.

with a common platform giving a cross-functional view of how the individual departments of the firm potentially can contribute to secure the firm a winning position by taking market leadership within and across the customer universes identified.

Summing up CUBEical strategy

In this chapter, an understanding of firms has been created matching the one developed for customers. With this CUBEical relationship framework at hand, customer universes and the firm universe can be discussed in matching terms and concepts. A consistent framework for understanding both, customers and the firm in question, is established.

CUBEical strategy is a four-step process as illustrated in Figure 7.8. After establishing the customer universes, adding current, as-is information on customer satisfaction and firm performance develops the foundation for opportunity development. Assessing and prioritizing the opportunities provides the platform for assigning opportunities to customer types and thereby for developing the CUBEical strategy represented by the customer strategy maps and market strategy map. These maps illustrate the strategy of the firm which provides the highest possible yield from the scarce resources employed.

For each chosen opportunity and unchanged arena, firms can now establish detailed reasoning and plans in a highly structured way. Figure 7.9 illustrates such a typical framework to be included in the roadmap documentation of the firm.

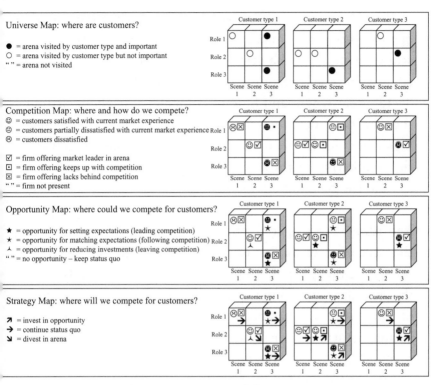

Figure 7.8   Overview of the maps.

Competitive arena strategy for	Customer type:	
	Role:	
	Scene:	
Competitive arena description	Opportunity	
Current market leader	ROI	
Current own position	Strategy	

Figure 7.9   Typical strategy description.

CUBEical strategy is about identifying and prioritizing market opportunities and arenas to be left unchanged against the scarce resources of the firm: A systematic balancing of market effectiveness and resource effectiveness. A strategy is about deciding on where and how to compete. It is about utilizing the firm's competencies in order to find ways to provide offerings which fulfill the needs of the customers and which drive the marketplace through setting customers´ expectations beyond the reach of competition.

Regarding where to compete, CUBEical strategy is addressing the executive agenda on profitable revenue growth by founding the strategy on the business opportunities identified for the served, as well as of the not yet served, competitive arenas of the firm. As it has been the theme throughout the book, strategy starts and ends with the customers. And profitable revenue growth does not stop at strategy – it needs implementation; our theme for the next chapter.

8

CUBEical implementation – how to take the lead

C UBEical implementation is about ensuring that the organization is equipped with the required tools and business procedures to transform the customer strategy maps into market success. Firms can significantly improve their performance by applying the tools and business procedures described in this chapter. We will explore the following five areas critical to implementation and, thus, to successfully targeting customers and guiding them through the AIDA process:

1. Customer profitability;

2. Selling process;

3. Mass communication;

4. Cross- and up-selling;

5. CRM framework.

Customer profitability

The developed strategy consists of setting the overall agenda for the firm on where and how to compete. It specifies how the firm will pursue its ambitions of generating profitable revenue growth. Generating profitable revenue growth is only possible through selling. The firm's market strategy map points out where, how, what and to whom to sell.

In the above, to whom refers to a customer type, not to an individual customer. All customers belonging to a specific customer type are homogeneous regarding their behaviors and ways of making decisions. But regarding their individual profitability they will typically differ significantly. Aiming for profitable revenue growth firms want to outgrow competition and their own customer portfolio in terms of profit, instead of just being very busy producing a lot of products for no additional profit.

Consider Figure 8.1: The white area exemplifies the customer portfolio of a firm for a given customer type. Without taking profitability of the individual customers into account, the firm can only grow across its full customer base for the given customer type. The best guess is that the firm will grow proportionally to its existing customer base. Herewith, as indicated by the vertical striped area, the firm is likely to grow significantly around the zero profit line – becoming extremely busy and growing revenues but not profits. Actually, this is not the most likely case to materialize when firms grow their customer base while not considering customer profitability. In reality, loss-giving customers will grow faster for the simple reason that bad customers are the

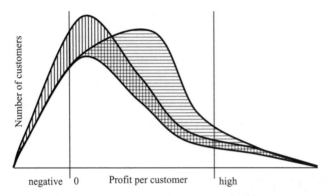

Figure 8.1 Profitable revenue growth vs. unprofitable revenue growth.

easiest to get because competitors try to get rid of them. These customers come running to a firm, not because they are enthusiastic about joining but because they are pushed out by other suppliers.

Firms pursuing profitable revenue growth must target profitable customers within a given customer type and assign service level standards to these based on a traditional ABC grouping of the customers. Profitability guided implementation ensures profitable revenue growth as illustrated by the horizontally striped area. Despite its simplicity, the 20/80 rule applies to most firms meaning that only 20% of the customers accounts for 80% of the profit. This rule still applies with segmentation of customers according to customer types, roles and scenes.

Thus, any implementation must start with the assessment of profitability per customer. Firms need profitable customers to drive growth – customers who generate value to the firm. This is not the same as saying that ABC grouping can replace good segmentation. As pointed out in Chapter 3, identifying profitable customers is not sufficient for driving growth because customer needs and expectations remain unclear. For driving sales, firm's profits do not configure in the mind of the customers, other than as an argument for pushing prices down. Firms need to present valid and valuable arguments to their profitable customers in order to sell their products.

Selling process

When implementing the customer strategy map, it is a pre-requisite for success that firms carefully consider if their current approach to sales fully leverages the customer insights. The customer strategy maps and all the underlying insights gained so far are worthless if a firm does not get the interaction with its customers right. When in contact, firms must explain themselves and their offerings to customers in a way customers understand. Speaking the customers' language has been discussed for a long time but implementation has been hindered due to a lack of insights into customers' minds. Therefore, the old wisdom has prevailed for a long time: Half of all sales and marketing costs are a waste of resources, but which half?

Based on segmenting customers according to customer types, roles and scenes, firms are now in the position to address what is on the customer's mind. Based on the strategic decision of how to serve the customer, documented in the customer strategy map, a firm communicates and delivers value to their customers by providing offerings which address a customer need. Thus, selling starts with the specific customer and the specific situation and links this insight to the firm's offering. This CUBEical selling approach reverses the argumentation of traditional product selling approaches (Figure 8.2).

What is the difference between product selling and CUBEical selling when a firm survives from selling its products anyway? The difference is small but has a major impact. Exchanging products, i.e. delivering goods and services, is the basis for gaining something in return from customers, mainly financial means. Being allowed to exchange products, i.e. closing a deal with a customer, has little to do with the product itself. Customers are not interested in products. They are interested in satisfying their needs, solving their problems, getting the job done. As another old marketing saying states: "There is no market for drilling machines but holes in walls are in demand." And this is only partially correct: No one wants holes in walls, but many want an attractive living room with paintings on the walls, or a whiteboard in a conference room, etc. Thus, product selling is one major reason why half of the sales and marketing expenses do not return any sales.

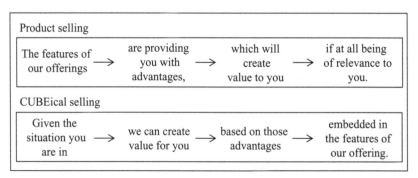

Figure 8.2   Product selling versus CUBEical selling.

Sales and marketing people know that they can sell only when they talk the customers' language both in terms of words and expressions used and in terms of making the product relevant to the customer. But with inadequate customer segmentation at hand and thereby not knowing what is on the customers' minds, sales people are left with guessing and making fools of themselves by talking nonsense, as seen by customers. Sales people solve this problem by talking about something safe, the product and its features. They turn to product selling and rely on the fact that the customers themselves will translate the features into something of value for them. Once that happens, and the sales person notices it, the sales person will immediately change the focus of the dialog towards these items of interest. Thus, the typical sales pitch is a collection of slides with all features of the product – and, if lucky, something will catch to interest of the customer.

As sales people are aware of the limitation of product and feature selling, they turn to the next level and start talking about the advantages the features of the offering potentially have for a customer. The 3.0 liter engine of a BMW X5 gives customers the advantage of accelerating faster and driving faster as compared to the 2.0 liter engine of the BMW X3. Such advantages may be translated into benefits for the customer. Here the talk finally arrives at the customer universe. The advantages of the 3.0 liter engine are better acceleration when overtaking and shorter travel times.

Is this interesting for a car buyer? Yes, for some it is. To speak in stereotypes, the young and wild may love the acceleration, the pressed-for-time business executive will benefit from the shorter travel time. But, maybe the customer needs the acceleration to pull a trailer. And the shorter travel time is meaningless due to traffic jams. However, the comfortable seats are interesting. If only sales people could know what is on the customers' minds, they could address a real and relevant problem.

The steps in product selling are outlined in the upper part of Figure 8.2. First, the customer is informed about the features and advantages provided by the offering. Then, the sales presentation outlines how the offering will create value for the customer – all under the assumption that the offering eventually addresses the needs and expectations of the customer. No wonder that half of the marketing and sales budgets are spent without results.

With CUBEical selling, the sales presentation changes radically. The customer strategy maps point out customer differences and how to differentiate the offering. The maps point out winning positions within the competitive arenas of importance. If customer type, roles and scenes are not already known, killer questions are at hand to quickly determine the customer type and competitive arena which is of interest for the customer. Thus, a sales person can address a customer's needs by speaking the customer's language. This expressed understanding of the customer's needs immediately builds trust. The sales talk can continue to describe the benefits of the suggested solution for the customer and link these to the advantages of the offering and, further, to product features. The direct and logical link between customer needs and product features creates credibility on top of the already created trustworthiness.

Compared to the way firms previously have been driving sales, the firm's ability to make sales messages relevant to customers is the winning formula for creating growth. From our experience implementing CUBEical selling has immediate and significant effects on generating profitable revenue growth.

Growing new customers

Especially when working with prospective customers, our clients have expressed great experiences with CUBEical selling. A typical scenario is: You should have seen the customer's face after our presentation. He was stunned by our insight into his business and the key points we highlighted were so important to him. He said: "Finally a supplier who understands my business. And all that without working with us before. I think we should talk through your proposal in detail – I hear we are on the same page."

Growing existing customers

Up-sales initiatives, i.e. selling more volume or higher-end products to a customer, have been very much in focus in recent years when the wave of single sourcing agreements washed through industry. The winner takes it all – but who is winning? The likelihood of winning increases significantly by talking the customer's language and addressing customer needs, and by simply understanding the customer universe and sharing this understanding with customers. In addition, projecting the firm's own competencies against customer needs into the future creates a sound and trustworthy basis for long-term decisions like single sourcing.

CUBEical selling solves the basic sales challenge of communicating effectively with customers in order to win their hearts and minds. But three more challenges remain to be solved in order to ensure that the customer strategies are being successfully implemented.

The first challenge is about the market efficiency of the firm's branding and mass communications. In addition to the many personal encounters, customers are also reachable via mass communication means. TV and radio spots, print advertisement, outdoor, in-shop, sponsoring, product placement – our world is filled with advertisements and public relations materials. But most of it does not make an impact. Firms need to effectively communicate with potential and existing customers by means of branding and mass communications. Increasing effectiveness of mass communication is explained in the next part of this chapter.

The second challenge is breaking down the organizational silos, typically characterizing sales organizations, for driving profitable revenue growth through cross-sales, i.e. widening the product portfolio sold to a customer. While up-sales initiatives are in the hands of those sales people already having a relationship with the customer (it is business as usual, just more of it), cross-sales often require cooperation across different sales units. The typical pattern is that once the sale is over, the deal is made, bonus is paid, everybody is happy. But, of course, it should not be so! We have seen so many firms that did sell something to a customer but it was by far not everything that they could have sold. Thus, many firms can realize tremendous growth rates in revenues by focusing on cross-selling. This is not innovation driven. Cross-sales are driven by understanding the existing product portfolio of the firm and simply selling all relevant products and product groups that are addressing customers' needs.

The third challenge concerns designing CRM systems to support daily operations and thus guiding the up- and cross-sales initiatives aimed at driving profitable growth. Knowing how to sell must be effectively supported by knowing what to sell. The customer strategy maps already specify the "what" but for efficient daily implementation, CRM systems must support the work of customer-facing employees.

Mass communication

Mass communication is typically applied to lead customers into the AIDA process (Figure 8.3). Thus, mass communications are a major focus of firms, and a major expense, especially in relation to corporate branding and product branding. Despite tracking and impact studies, mass communications are often seen as esoteric activities with doubtful impact. Many firms actually use mass communication because their competitors do. Asked for the impact made, they do not expect too much. A common statement is that customers apparently have lost interest in mass communication. TV viewers switch channels when commercials are shown, newspaper readers do not usually look at printed advertisements but if they do it is only for a few seconds, and people in cities do not even

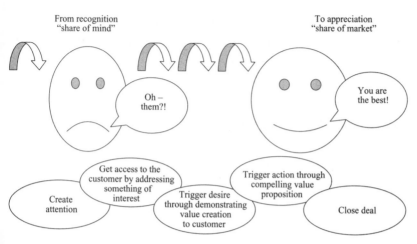

Figure 8.3 The AIDA model.

remember that there was something on that bus, that wall or that billboard – they are not even sure if there was a bus, a wall or billboard. Still, firms keep on increasing the noise level in the marketplace by sending out obscure communications about their goods and services, despite their conviction that mass communication has lost its impact. Maybe customers lost interest because mass communications are irrelevant for customers most of the time.

Asked for reasons why they use a significant amount of money each year for low impact marketing activities, they say: What do you expect from a mass channel? We send an average message to the market and hope to hit widely within our target group.

This is exactly the root problem of much mass communication material today – average messages. Customers are different and no single customer is average. Let's try to overcome the average message problem by addressing two points: Increase the ambition level and discuss differentiation potential in mass communication.

Increase the ambition level

Many firms know that their mass communication barely leaves the first A in the AIDA model (Figure 8.3): Mass communication creates awareness that the firm is still doing business. As such, the ambition for a communication campaign is that customers can recall the brand, unaided or aided. The sheer happiness high unaided brand recall numbers are producing in marketing departments is unbelievable. Of course, customers must be aware of a firm before they can decide to buy something from them. While the aim of communication is to produce a customer, awareness is necessary but not sufficient.

Billions of marketing dollars are spent on communication campaigns that brand a firm into a group of firms where all firms appear to be the same in the eyes of the customer. The numbers in Figure 8.4 apply to many firms. Customers are satisfied and would even recommend the firm to friends and colleagues. But customers cannot see the difference between firms. What is the actual difference between the car rental firms Avis, Eurocar, Hertz and Sixt? They all have the same cars, their prices and conditions are look-alikes, and their desks are located within 200 meters of each other. And their loyalty programs are also close to being identical. This is not a basis for customer loyalty. Loyalty in this context is a nice illusion, something for daydreaming.

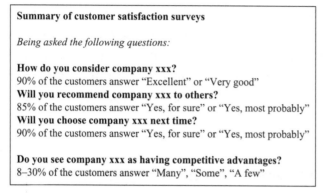

Figure 8.4 Typical satisfaction and competitive advantage scores.

The numbers basically indicate that customers are indifferent rather than satisfied and that retention has more to do with customers not being motivated to leave as opposed to customers being urged to stay due to deep felt loyalty. Thus, such numbers should make firms realize that they don't belong to the small privileged group of firms, finding themselves clearly differentiated from competitors.

Many firms are being caught undifferentiated. They know that mass communication too often misses its targets: Differentiation and making customers buy. When asked about this problem, campaigns are described as image campaigns and reminder messages. So driving a customer along the AIDA process has apparently never been the ambition for mass communication.

If this low ambition level is accepted, many marketing resources can be saved by just stopping mass communication. If awareness is the only ambition, why do firms with awareness levels close to 100% advertise? Everybody knows these firms. But many "100% awareness" firms have an astonishing gap between their market recognition and their market share (Figure 8.5). Many customers apparently drop out of the AIDA process. Thus, the ambition for a significant number of firms is not to increase mind share but to increase market share.

Differentiation potential in mass marketing

Mass communications often tend to position the firm in a cluster of peers and not as a shining star, because firms lack the insights into how the firm's corporate values translate into the minds of the customers, the customer types. Only if customers understand and associate themselves with the firm's type will the foundation for true loyalty be present. Therefore, to be market efficient corporate branding must be based on a sequence of messages tailored to the individual customer types.

When mass communications start mirroring the fact that customers differ, firms pull themselves out of the cluster of undifferentiated peers. The firm differentiates itself clearly

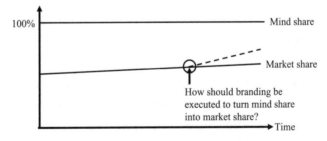

Figure 8.5 Market recognition vs. market share.

from competition as it signals how it adapts its behaviors and ways of making decisions to match those of the individual customer types. This differentiation is successful when two criteria are fulfilled:

- Mass communications must target individual customer types and relevant situations – this makes messages under-standable and meaningful to customers;

- Mass communications must translate the firm's compe-tencies and offerings into relevant expectations about solving customer needs. Preferably, customer expectations are set beyond the reach of competition.

These requirements cannot be fulfilled with average mes-sages. The alternative to making one-size-fits-all mass com-munication showing products is showing different customer types. With this approach, differences between customers are mirrored in differences between characters in the advertise-ments. When being presented to the communication mate-rial, customers will tune into their own customer type. Hereby, the customers become involved as they, from their own perspectives, reflect on the situation they are being exposed to through the communication.

For example, the Danish railway operator DSB has been very successful in introducing the purple, red-haired puppet Harry who prefers his car, and his DSB enthusiast friend Bahnsen, played by a well-known Danish actor. The commer-cials display Harry and Bahnsen in different situations in which the two argue about their different views of DSB. Harry touts the advantages of his old beat-up car while

Bahnsen, who always goes by the train, argues in favor of trains being faster, cheaper and more efficient. The Harry commercials are recalled better compared to other commercials. Eighty-nine percent of the Danish population between 15 and 59 years of age like the commercials. The campaign has been reported to give back 4.9 times the investment.

Differentiation works – also in mass communication. The success formula of the commercials is simple: Do not create an average message but two significantly different messages which span the whole market universe – two customer types, across commercials in various roles and scenes. Address real needs and show how the firm solves them. Make it entertaining but not pure entertainment (some firms seem to forget that commercials are about selling and not about pure entertainment).

The precision offered by customer types, roles and scenes also shifts the power balance between firms and their media and advertising agencies. Firms with customer insight take the driver's seat and the responsibility for communications to its customers. With descriptions of customer types, competitive arenas and the corporate values of the firm, targeting communication, making messages relevant and selecting the right media are made more transparent. Also, the result of creative work and media planning suggestions can be discussed based on insights as opposed to feelings.

The opportunities for increasing the market efficiency of communication become evident when marketing adapts a differentiated view on mass communications. By changing the ambition level and using customer insight, efficient marketing communications can be implemented.

Cross- and up-selling

For the ambition of profitable revenue growth to materialize during implementation, firms need to find these profitable customers which have not yet bought all the products they could buy from the firm's total product portfolio. Through the segmentation process, customers are assigned their respective customer type. Therewith, firms are in the position to compare customers with similar needs and expectations in terms of what they buy from the firm.

Typically, there is a high correlation between customer type and products purchased (Figure 8.6). Also, there is a hierarchy, as not all products are equally important to customers. Through sales of a few key products within a product group, a sales person gains a foothold for maintaining an ongoing dialog with the customer. This is a natural platform for contacting the customer every now and then, and a platform for an open minded dialog.

Mapping of goods and services to customer types is just as straightforward as all other steps within the CUBEical framework. Thus, CUBEical implementation is a framework for sharing and leveraging upon the experience gained from the best in class customer relationship for a given customer type.

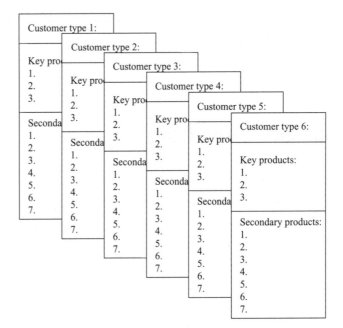

Figure 8.6 Allocating products and services to customer types.

The customers representing the broadest portfolio purchased within and across the product groups of the firm build the basis for sales efforts to other customers.

With such a product overview at hand (Figure 8.7), a sales person can identify the cross-sales opportunities not yet being harvested. Furthermore, by drilling down in the product groups (Figure 8.6), the sales person can plan the specific cross-sales initiative as to which goods and services to sell. Likewise, the sales person can determine if there are any not yet harvested up-sales opportunities left.

Of course, there can be good explanations for why a given customer shows slightly different demand patterns compared

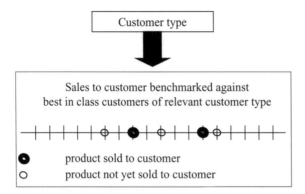

Figure 8.7 Identifying cross-sales opportunities for a customer belonging to a given customer type.

to those of the best in class customers, but generally the product overview (Figure 8.7) exposes areas where up- and cross-sales potential ought to be harvested. There is a huge potential in driving profitable revenue growth by activating the up- and cross-sales potentials. Most often we see clients realizing two-digit revenue growth rates.

But how come responsible sales people tend to forget to expose their customers to the product groups of relevance to the customer in question? What makes the sales person leave the customer to competitors for products handled by the sales person's colleagues?

Unaddressed cross-sales opportunities are typically linked to firm size: Bigger firms are more prone to the forgotten sales syndrome and tend to have product specialists who for organizational reasons sit in different units. Thus, sales people have their favorite products – the ones they know most about. And sales people have their customer relationships, meaning that no other person is allowed to contact their customers. In combination, these two items lead to a situation where only a part of the firm's product portfolio is offered to customers – the rest is simply forgotten.

As for cross-sales, the challenge in making the implementation of the customer strategy maps successful is to break down the silos often characterizing product-driven sales organizations. Here the individual sales people, due to the lack of a vehicle for knowledge sharing, store all valuable customer information in their heads. Consequently, they are the ones who own the customer. The incentives to drive cross-sales through letting sales people represent other groups of goods and services are few, if at all present. Most often sales people are evaluated based on individual performance or on the group's performance as to the sales of the group's products. Facing the potential risk of jeopardizing the customer relationship by introducing a colleague from another sales silo, organized cross-sales is the exemption, not the rule.

As to the cross-sales process, the sales person having the best relationship with a customer should be made responsible for keeping track of the products and services sold. In addition, this person should also be responsible for deciding on the next step in cross-sales. Which new group of products and services should be exposed to the customer and what is considered to be the best approach?

Cross-selling is about breaking down silos. Cross-sales are performed in a corporation between the sales person being in contact with the customer and the sales person who is intending to make the sale of a product not yet taken on board by the customer, i.e. one colleague representing the product group silo and another the profit center. The cross-sales procedure is outlined in Figure 8.8.

Having identified a cross-sales opportunity, the sales person owning the relationship contacts the product specialist to handle the sale. First, the two must agree that the opportunity identified is worth pursuing. Thereafter, the sales person is briefed by the product specialist about how the interest of the customer can be triggered and the information which would be required for preparing a meeting with the customer regarding the cross-sales opportunity.

Once the sales person has opened the door and collected the preliminary information about the specific situation the customer is in, the responsibility for the cross-sale process is handed over to the product specialist. Having been introduced, the product specialist can now call the customer to ask for more information before actually meeting the

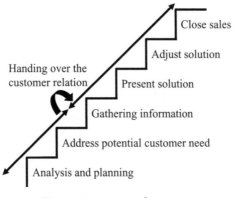

Figure 8.8 Cross-sales steps.

customer. Hereby, when the meeting takes place the information-gathering stage is over and the meeting will typically be about presenting and adjusting a solution to the needs and expectations of the customer.

Once a cross-sale has been successfully closed, the next initiative may start. From our experience it is recommended only to run one or few cross-sales initiatives towards a customer at a time and it is furthermore recommended that these campaigns should not interfere with the day-to-day business with the customer.

Once implemented, the customer-facing employees become very enthusiastic about driving cross-sales. One driver is learning about the product portfolio as addressed in Figure 8.6, another is learning about how the individual goods and services within the portfolio are creating value for the customer type in question. Being aware of situations where the best in class customers of a given customer type have prospered from the firm's offerings, sales people feel encouraged to share such good stories with similar customers who have not yet taken these offerings on board.

In our experience, targeted up- and cross-sales initiatives drive profitable revenue growth at extraordinarily high growth rates. Increasing the firm's share of a customer's wallet is, on the one hand, about selling by ensuring that all offerings within a given group of goods and services are taken on board by the customer. On the other hand, growing the share of wallet is also about cross-sales, i.e. selling in all relevant groups of goods and services to the customer in question. Furthermore, the management of sales people changes.

Coaching sales people turns into targeted meetings where the sales person's account plan is discussed based on the benchmark of the customer in question against best in class.

Not performing cross-sales can actually be considered poor customer service. If a customer has a demand which can be fulfilled by the firm, leaving the customer to the competition is letting the customer down! Hereby, CUBEical selling radically sharpens the competitive attitude within sales. Either the firm is competitive and therefore cutting off the competition, or sales must revisit the competitive arenas to figure out how the firm can change its strategy to become competitive.

CRM framework

For leveraging existing customer relationships and existing product competence, driving up- and cross-sales efficiently typically requires some kind of CRM system support. To efficiently drive up- and cross-sales the firm needs information about:

- Customer type;

- Number and value of products and services sold;

- Customer profitability;

- Firmographic or demographic customer characteristics;

- Share of wallet.

Customer type is assigned to the customer based on the segmentation process. The number and value of goods and services sold are general transaction data. Profitability can generally be calculated based on sales and on the service level agreement associated with the customer type in question. As customer types typically cut across firmo-graphics and demographics, sometimes product portfolios can be more precisely defined when including demo-firmo-graphic parameters; e.g. in some industries it is necessary for the materials employed to have a certificate while in other industries this isn't required. Share of wallet is often employed to estimate the additional business potential of a customer.

Having access to the basic set of data described above, best in class portfolios can be established by taking the product groups and associated goods and services typically sold to the top 10 customers within a given customer type, with the same size of wallet, same range of profitability, and the same demo-firmo-graphics.

Having these best in class customers established and updated on an ongoing basis within the CRM system, sales people can immediately obtain the up- and cross-sales information required to drive profitable revenue growth (Figure 8.9).

The specific CRM set-up for identifying up- and cross-sales initiatives is firm and industry specific. Generally, the data required is already at hand and the functionality required is what is available in simple spreadsheet applications.

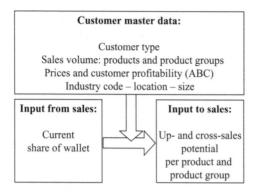

Figure 8.9   CRM framework for driving cross-sales.

Summing up CUBEical implementation

In this chapter on CUBEical implementation we focused our attention on the implementation of the customer-facing activities of the strategy map. Firms find it difficult getting to grips with these activities as compared to internal activities. Regarding sales, profitable revenue growth was introduced, pointing out the need for focusing on increasing sales to customers with above average profits while at the same time getting rid of customers eroding EBITDA. ABC customer ranking was introduced as a way of keeping track of customer profitability within the individual customer types.

Thereafter, CUBEical selling was introduced as the vehicle for making sales messages relevant to customers. Mass communications provide an important contribution to the AIDA process through which marketing and sales together pursue the maximization of market efficiency of their activities.

Therefore, it was discussed how firms can increase market efficiency by applying CUBEical Thinking to their mass communications activities.

Finally, we discussed how up- and cross-sales represent a huge, unharvested potential for profitable revenue growth. Following this concept, it was discussed how up- and cross-sales can best be driven by benchmarking customers against best in class. It was discussed how cross-sales can be implemented within an organization and how they can be supported by the firm's CRM system.

PART III
Living the customer universe

In previous chapters, we developed a business management framework for running a firm in a way which is characterized by Customer Universe Based Execution – in short, CUBEical. The focus was on a firm and its customers. We described a structured way to discover the customer universe by introducing three dimensions – customer types, roles and scenes. This structure was then deployed to analyze customers and competitors in order to develop a firm strategy about how to deal with its customers to achieve maximum EBITDA results. Further, we described how the gained customer insight is used to efficiently drive selling and mass communication as well as realizing up- and cross-selling potential.

In this final part of the book, we first explain how the different frameworks interact and how they together build the CUBEical Thinking framework. CUBEical Thinking is a framework for making customers the pivotal focus on the executive agenda of driving profitable revenue growth. It is compatible with other management concepts and adds to the insights they provide by structuring customer knowledge.

The perspective taken in this book so far is one of a firm and its direct customers, whereby the customer is seen as one unit. While this view of business fits nicely and offers a number of insights, reality is not always that simple. Often, firms do not work directly with their customers but work through intermediaries, distributors, agents, or other forms of middlemen. Technically, these middlemen are the customers, and it is sufficient to understand their way of thinking. But often, insight into customers' customers is required. Therefore, we explain a typical set-up of middlemen and how CUBEical Thinking works in such layered systems. We have chosen the fast moving consumer goods manufacturer–retailer–consumer chain to explain the framework's contribution.

Also, a customer is seldom just one customer. Especially in business markets, firms have multiple contact points with their customer. Thus, we explore CUBEical in terms of account management. Even though we describe a business-to-business market setting in the account management chapter, consumer markets also feature multi-person decisions: Buying houses and cars, booking holidays, deciding on schools, etc. As such, the account management logic also applies to these settings.

And, finally, a firm is seldom just one firm. It is often a collection of business units which are aligned with each other at varying degrees. The collection of business units becomes very visible when new business units are added and the interfaces need to be defined. We therefore address the challenges of aligning business units in relation to mergers and acquisitions.

9

CUBEical Thinking – how it links to other business frameworks

C UBEICAL THINKING IS A FRAMEWORK FOR FIRMS TO successfully develop and implement their market leader strategies. CUBEical Thinking is about revealing and leveraging upon the most valuable asset of the firm, namely the customer knowledge held by the customer-facing employees. The framework consists of three pillars introduced in previous chapters (Figure 9.1): Segmentation (Chapter 6), strategy (Chapter 7) and implementation (Chapter 8):

- CUBEical segmentation is the vehicle for harvesting and sharing knowledge about customers across the organization by applying customer types, roles and scenes.

- CUBEical strategy provides the foundation for leveraging upon customer knowledge by developing differentiated market leader strategies which set customer expectations beyond the reach of competition.

- CUBEical implementation provides the firm with the tools for demonstrating, communicating and creating value to their customers by successfully implementing differentiated customer strategies.

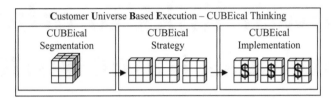

Figure 9.1 CUBEical Thinking business management framework.

What is left to discuss after having shown the way to profitable revenue growth? Not much, of course. But still, there are other challenges in running a firm which are positively affected by CUBEical Thinking.

One major issue in many firms is intellectual capital, primarily issues surrounding the tacit knowledge of employees are important. Tacit knowledge is per definition only accessible by the owner of that knowledge. If formally shared, for example between employees of a department, it is no longer tacit, it is explicit. Firms are very aware of their explicit knowledge and eager to secure that important explicit knowledge is not transferred to competitors or other third parties as this can present a major threat to the firm. However, if knowledge stays tacit, the organization cannot leverage on that knowledge because the capacity of the owner limits its use. As such, firms have a strong interest in explicating tacit knowledge in order to make it accessible for other employees to enable leverage and growth while at the same time trying to keep it inaccessible for competitors.

In the first part of this chapter, we will explore how CUBEical Thinking links into the concept of knowledge management and enables organizational learning. We will discuss how the ambition of making customers the pivotal focus on the executive agenda of driving profitable revenue growth neatly links into the agenda on managing and leveraging upon the intellectual capital of the firm to maximize returns to shareholders.

Having positioned CUBEical Thinking within knowledge management and shareholder value, we conclude this chapter by linking our framework to developments in management concepts applied by firms over the last three decades. Our main argument is that CUBEical Thinking interlinks with these concepts and adds the missing piece to the EBITDA puzzle the customer universe.

CUBEical Thinking and knowledge management

As noted in Chapter 2, it is a paradox that customers are at the forefront of executives' minds while also at the outskirts of their agenda when it comes to driving EBITDA. We concluded that executives have optimized their firm's EBITDA, focusing on resource efficiency, while the lack of market efficiency initiatives rests on inadequate customer segmentation. The reason for a lack of customer focus is not a lack of knowledge. Firms know their customers. The discussion and implementation of CUBEical segmentation actually rests on knowledge held by customer-facing employees. These

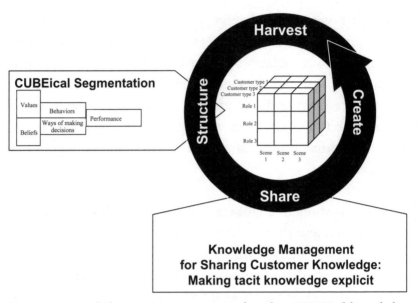

Figure 9.2 Knowledge management process based on CUBEical knowledge structure.

employees can easily identify customer types, they can in detail describe the interactions taking place within the competitive arenas. Customer knowledge is created every day. Firms know and have probably always known much more about their customers than they would ever believe. Knowledge generation is not the problem – there is plenty inside any firm. So what is the problem? Let's consider the four-step knowledge management process (Figure 9.2):

1. Firms need to *create knowledge*. In our case, knowledge is created by experiencing customers, thus the focus on customer-facing employees. Herewith, firms deal with experiential knowledge which is often tacit.

2. Firms need to *harvest knowledge*. It is not enough to plant seeds and grow plants; a farmer needs to harvest the crop as well. Likewise, firms need to find ways of harvesting the tacit knowledge of their employees.

3. Firms need to *structure knowledge*. In a world of information overflow, more information does not help, it actually confuses even more. Information becomes knowledge when being made explicit and documented in a structure which gives meaning to the recipient and allows efficient search in the wealth of information. Structure is important.

4. Firms need to *share knowledge*, i.e. share the structured knowledge base and use the knowledge. The application of shared knowledge leads to leverage – not only a buzz-word, but a necessity for achieving business results.

After sharing, employees have new knowledge and see the world slightly differently. They create new knowledge based on the new insights but also on the fact that our world is dynamic. New knowledge is created every day through the interactions with customers. There is always something new – knowledge management is an ever-turning wheel. As the knowledge management process is logical and simple, what makes knowledge management so difficult to handle in practice?

As mentioned, it is not creation of knowledge. Firms know their customers: Some better than others, but in general solid customer knowledge is with customer-facing employees. Regarding harvesting, many firms struggle to get to grips with their knowledge about customers. CRM software has not made this problem disappear. Firms implemented CRM systems in order to put the knowledge of their employees into a database but these projects apparently have been facing fundamental problems:

First, data content (you know, the field you may fill in) did not allow for important things to be registered. Seldom are we confronted with CRM systems that register more than demo-firmo-graphics (names, positions, education level, address, size, age, income and turnover), ABC grouping (sales volume, product mix) and sales history (order chronology, contact history). We have already explained the problems with using these types of information for customer insight in Chapter 3.

Second, as the data entries represent already explicit knowledge with limited additional value to the individual, there is often a general resistance among employees to enter data into the system. The often heard remark, "could we instead get a system integrating our mail and calendar with the customer database then we would be happy", tells something about the business value of the typical data held in CRM systems.

Third, the structure is missing. Information is just dumped into the system never to be found and used again. These fields are often called "free text" but in practice are "free of structure". The data set-up is not intuitively understandable because the data structure is not linked to the business framework outlining how customers are to be served. Consequently, despite a great deal of effort being spent on user training on how to use the system, it is soon forgotten.

Finally, leveraging implies not only finding but also understanding information. The understanding of knowledge depends heavily on the understanding of the context and the sender of the knowledge. Looking for soccer results, it helps to know where to look (structure). The figures "0-2" mean nothing; knowing that it is a soccer score adds some context; knowing that it is the final result of a game between Germany and Italy adds even more; and knowing that it was the semifinal at the Soccer World Cup in 2006 adds the necessary context to understanding the information.

As there are many barriers on the way, it is not surprising that firms leapfrog the process and let the people who generate the knowledge organize their own knowledge about customers for themselves. Beyond the efficiency of such implementations in the short run, these solutions create a multitude of individual solutions and are very vulnerable. If an employee is absent from work no one else can serve that employee's customers properly. If an employee leaves the firm, his or her knowledge is lost because the knowledge has been structured for personal use only and remains tacit. In such cases, customers will say: "They have completely lost it. It is like they have never done this before. We have to teach them all over again how things should be." A solid base of customer dissatisfaction is created.

Harvesting, structuring and, thus, sharing of customer knowledge seems to be the problem. Employees are generally motivated to open their minds but firms miss a structure to fill in the knowledge. The missing link for firms to benefit from their customer knowledge is a good customer segmentation framework for structuring customer knowledge. Current segmentation practices have created more confusion than clarity to structuring customer knowledge because all too many segmentation models are not living up to good segmentation practice. In contrast to reality, customers have become moving targets in segmentation models and, thus, in CRM databases. As long as they are moving, customer knowledge cannot be leveraged upon as the customer knowledge cannot be structured or shared. The knowledge remains tacit and only the good sales people can access it, without actually realizing the value of the knowledge held by them. For them, selling is easy and they just do what they do.

When running client workshops, it is our experience that customer-facing employees are highly motivated to share their knowledge provided they see that sharing is bringing benefits to themselves, their customers, their colleagues and the firm. In general, customer-facing employees enjoy talking about their experiences with customers – because it is their day-to-day business, because they like being experts, because they appreciate that others show real interest in their work – and last but not least, because they find it is great fun to realize the tremendous reach of their own customer knowledge. Knowledge sharing does not have to be a pain.

Based on the three dimensions of customer types, roles and scenes making up the customer universes with associated competitive arenas, CUBEical segmentation lives up to good segmentation practice. Hereby, the derived knowledge structure is intuitively understandable and knowledge is readily being created during the interactions with customers. The created structure of knowledge enables the process.

CUBEical Thinking business management framework

For leveraging knowledge, the knowledge base needs to be utilized. In Chapter 8, we have demonstrated how structured customer knowledge can be used to systematically improve interactions with customers in three ways: Selling to customers based on what is relevant to them, communicating with customers again based on what is relevant to them, and knowing the relevant product portfolio to offer. These impacts of customer knowledge are positive for customers because they get better communications and more valuable offerings. Customer knowledge-based implementation is also positive for the firm as sales and communications become more efficient and up- and cross-selling potential is better utilized.

Given resource restrictions and corporate visions of the future, knowledge-driven implementation needs to be guided by a strategy to achieve maximum effectiveness. Thus, let's quickly consider a typical strategy process in four steps. First, a firm's knowledge base is accessed. Necessary knowledge is identified and brought to the table. In case of missing knowledge, market research is conducted or experts brought into the firm. The next step is analyzing data. After analysis, a decision is made. And, finally, the decision is implemented. This process is illustrated as the outer process which runs simultaneously with the knowledge management process (Figure 9.3).

Unfortunately, simultaneously does not mean automatically synchronized. If the knowledge base is not accessible, e.g.

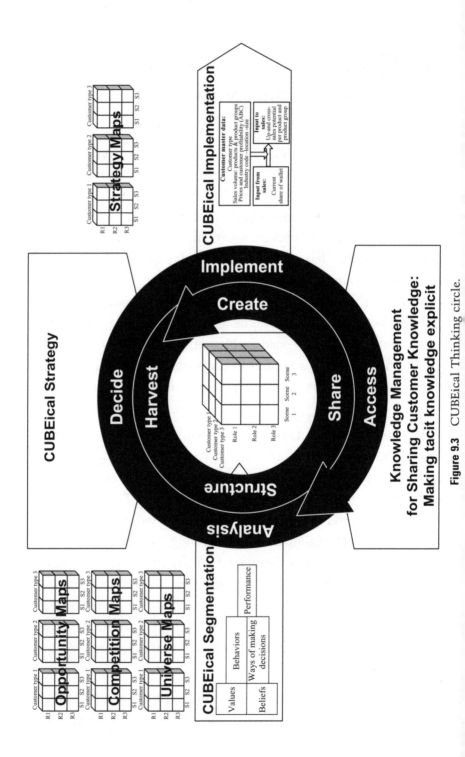

Figure 9.3 CUBEical Thinking circle.

because it is tacit knowledge, or explicit knowledge is not understandable because the structure is not developed, the strategy process is disconnected from knowledge and, thus, either has no impact or the wrong impact on implementation. Both situations are suboptimal. In the CUBEical Thinking framework, the leveraging process can commence as the customer knowledge held by the customer-facing employees is now within the knowledge base of the organization. It can be accessed by the other members of the organization and used for analysis because the knowledge base is understandable.

In particular, the executive agenda benefits from this accessibility of customer knowledge. Executives need access to knowledge in order to perform the analysis required to make sound decisions on which options to pursue. With CUBEical segmentation in place, customer knowledge is available. Because the context of the knowledge, the customer universe, is intuitively understandable, CUBEical segmentation enables analysis and decision-making. Executives understand their market and can talk about it in a language which is compatible with the knowledge and language across the organization.

Knowledge and decisions regarding segmentation, strategy and implementation are documented at the competitive arena level for each customer type. The customer and market competition maps illustrate the development of all as-is situations. Hereby, the progress of implementing the strategy is documented (how far are we in our implementation?), as well as the impact of the strategy (what did we achieve?). There is full transparency and traceability in all decisions made with regard to both laying the strategy and implementing it throughout the organization. The processes are not only transparent but also integrated. The results achieved in the market can be captured and reflected upon within the existing structure and, thus, made available for the next round of decision-making. This enables straight tracking of results and an understanding of what is best practice and what must be improved.

Herewith, CUBEical Thinking presents an intuitively under-standable, coherent and transparent framework for securing that relevant knowledge is harvested and structured as well as leveraged upon in order to achieve the targets set in the strategy. Implementation is about executing the strategy in order to generate profitable revenue growth through creating true customer loyalty and fulfilling customer expecta-tions – those expectations the firm has set beyond the reach of competitors.

The challenge for firms has been to create a common language enabling the organization to harvest, structure, share and, thus, to leverage upon the joint customer knowledge of the organization. Having such a language, customers can be made the pivotal focus on the executive agenda for driving profit-able revenue growth by increasing sales and marketing efficiency and increasing the understanding of customers by non customer-facing employees. Customer insight, strategy development and deployment, as well as sales and marketing, are all working with the same picture of the customer, the customer universes and the same database, the knowledge database of the universes.

Hereby, the segmentation framework serves as a mental market model of the firm, i.e. the frame of reference which all employees across the organization use for translating their tacit knowledge into explicit knowledge. The strength of the firm's mental model is that it fully resembles real customer behaviors and decision patterns mirrored in the specific combinations of roles and scenes, i.e. the competitive arena, where interactions take place. Thus, the mental models of individual employees are closely aligned to the mental model of the firm. It is this link which makes developing and implementing CUBEical Thinking effective. The familiarity of the mental model makes the segmentation framework an effective platform for sharing and communicating customer experiences across the organization. This contributes to continuous updating of the knowledge base by downloading tacit knowledge.

Applying the framework, tacit customer knowledge held by the customer-facing employees is turned into explicit knowledge which is available for strategy development input as well as for implementing the strategy at the individual customer level. At the individual customer level, the knowledge base and the strategy are converted into up- and cross-sales possibilities for generating profitable growth enabled by the CRM system.

Previously, the tacit knowledge of the customer-facing employees has been considered difficult to communicate, difficult to transfer and difficult to share with others because it is context specific and personal. Customer knowledge is built by customer-facing employees experiencing their customers. Firms cannot change the tacit nature of that knowledge and neither should they change it. The alternative is to rely purely on public knowledge which is restricted to demo-firmo-graphics. Firms should actually encourage their employees to encounter customer behavior.

What firms can change is their knowledge structure by developing a structure which mirrors the customer universes. Through the similarity of "real" customers and "database" customers, employees are motivated to use the system, to enrich data, to make it worthwhile. As soon as the knowledge structure is not an alien but a reasonable representation of reality, tacit knowledge can be unlocked and made explicit.

The knowledge created has been harvested, structured and shared by matching the mental model of customer-facing employees and the data model in the database. This match is achieved by letting the people with the mental model, the customer-facing people, develop the data model. What sounds logical on paper has been a major problem for firms. The framework and processes described in Part I are guiding the way to achieve this match. In a nutshell, the CUBEical Thinking framework guides the customer-facing employees in making sense of the strategy on an account level by using their own words and knowledge. It also allows executives to make customer-related decisions (are there decisions in firms which ultimately do not affect customers?) with an intuitive understanding of the matter.

The missing piece in the business puzzle of the past

The focus on EBITDA, profits, ROI, share prices, etc. is by no means new. Basically, this focus is what business is all about: Making money within the boundaries of law and social responsibility. A medieval trader, a manager in 2008, a factory owner in 1890 – whoever is in business, is in business to make a business. This does not imply that business people are not interested in employee welfare and societal matters. But they need to run a business.

Given this interest to improve business results, it is no surprise that management literature has continuously delivered new concepts aimed at supporting firms in improving their performance. The different pieces of advice have been made available to executives over time and one by one. Consequently, various pieces of the puzzle to improve EBITDA results came in shapes not compatible with each other. By implementing a new piece, firms experienced difficulties due to incompatibility. Just think of the ongoing discussions of decentralizing vs centralizing: after empowering business units firms strive for regaining control.

Staying in the puzzle metaphor, executives have been supplied with many pieces of a great puzzle but with no picture on the outside of the box showing how the picture should look once the puzzle is completed. Many firms are still struggling to complete the EBITDA puzzle and getting their profitability up to target, i.e. completing the puzzle toward a meaningful picture. Let's revisit some of the management concepts developed over the last decades and explore what is puzzling executives.

Five forces

Porter's five forces model has made a major impact on strategic planning. The model fits the executive requirements: The context of the model is easy to understand, executives know the difference between customers, suppliers, new entrants, internal rivalry and substitutes. The model offered accountability: Where are the major threats and impacts on EBITDA results coming from? Who has responsibility for dealing with this? And the model has a clear connection to results. If a firm can decrease the selling power of suppliers or the buying power of customers, profitability will increase.

Consequently, a firm's strategic options were to adapt to these forces in order to obtain above-average profits compared to the competitors within the industry, to try to change the rules of the game by changing the industry structure, or simply to pull out of the industry. Basically, the firm should position itself in the role it would play within its industry and thereafter optimize the efficiency of the capital employed. The assumption being that there is no need to segment customers, as they will simply recognize a firm's position and react accordingly, i.e. segment themselves.

The five forces model provides a strategic framework for analyzing and understanding the profitability of an *industry*. Still, today, many firms base their overall strategy on industry level analysis. This implies that they differentiate themselves from their competitors but assume a somewhat homogeneous customer base. We call this the *industry trap*. Firms captured by this trap downplay the importance of segmentation as an unnecessary expense given the homogeneity of their market. Why pay attention to something with no impact?

There is an inbuilt problem with industry thinking: A firm needs to create a customer, and can do so by differentiating its offerings towards this customer's needs and expectations. A firm does not exist to create a competitor by differentiating its offering towards the competitor. Of course, firms differentiate themselves from competitors. But this differentiation needs to be done from the customers' perspective. There is nothing worse for a customer than facing two truly differentiated firms which both do not offer what the customer wants. Profits are not driven by industry positions but by positioning the firm relative to customers and customer groups and by employing situation-specific views on customers.

CUBEical Thinking offers customer insight to understand internal rivalry at competitive arena and customer universe levels. Also, CUBEical Thinking integrates the five forces traditionally seen as five independent boxes. As explained in the strategy chapter, competitive arena requirements (the customers) are connected to the business set-up including suppliers.

Generic strategies

The industry trap creates a major problem for firms. Firms inevitably end up being "stuck in the middle" because of the gap between their general industry strategy and the needs of the different market segments. One size simply does not fit all. Instead of being something special to someone special, because of their generic positions firms become nothing special to no one special. And as all firms position themselves according to this logic, even branded companies find themselves "stuck in the middle" among peers who have spent equally huge amounts to build share the mind among the very same customers.

The industry trap of one generic strategy for a market or niche has yet another deficiency. Customers today employ increasingly single-source, or one-stop sourcing, strategies. This means that customers are not prepared to maintain relationships to one cost leader and a few differentiators (e.g. quality, volume and innovation suppliers). Customers wish to get it all from one source. So instead of choosing one role, firms are faced with demands of playing various roles at the same time. This is manifested in a change from key technology management to key account management. As such, generic industry strategies are unsuitable for today's customer relationship management initiatives and the one-stop-shopping solution.

Business process re-engineering (BPR) and enterprise resource planning (ERP)

Despite the strong focus on customers in the initial business process re-engineering literature, this focus was soon forgotten. The BPR piece of the puzzle supports an inward-looking perspective. The concept of BPR triggered a wave of "enterprise resource planning" (ERP) systems which paradoxically have kept firms in an internally focused iron grip during the last 20 years. The aim of the ERP systems was to provide transparency across the business processes of the firm and thereby enable seamless integration of all processes in order to minimize costs and optimize quality, service and speed.

Ironically, the idea of fundamentally rethinking and radically redesigning business processes to create customer and shareholder value ended up in "best practice processes" embedded in standardized ERP industry solutions, reinforced by uncontrollable costs of making changes to standard ERP systems. The development of the ERP systems took its departure in internal, non-customer-facing, processes such as finance, production, inventory and logistics. With these systems implemented, differentiated customer interaction becomes a nightmare, not a business model.

Customer relationship management (CRM)

During the last few years, firms have gradually started to extend their ERP systems to include customer-facing functions such as sales, marketing and service. The implementation of these customer relationship management (CRM) systems has to most firms been a painful experience. First, the experiences from ERP implementations of non-customer-facing processes could not be transferred to CRM implementations. When working with non-customer-facing processes the objectives were clear: Reduce throughput time by x%, reduce stock level by y%, bring down the time of issuing an invoice from 10 days to 1 day and so on. The task was to stretch the business to "best practice" processes and maximize the internal efficiency of the resources linked to the internal processes.

In contrast, the objectives of customer-facing processes are hard to make operational by taking them beyond general measures like increased sales, customer satisfaction and profits. Consequently, customer-facing business processes were re-engineered without clear objectives. The tacit customer knowledge required to maximize market efficiencies of the customer-facing activities remained tacit knowledge. Consequently, CRM implementations by far failed as the customer-facing employees' way of intuitively differentiating customers was replaced by rigidly streamlined, re-engineered and lean sales and marketing processes unable to support the needs and expectations of the customers.

The missing piece

We stop our little tour through management concepts here despite the fact that core competences, balanced score card, supply chain optimization, lean, Six Sigma, etc. could easily also be discussed. All concepts discussed here and those not discussed state the importance of customers. No serious business person and no business professor will ever neglect the importance of customers. So why did management concepts turn out not to focus on customers?

One simple reason is that some concepts do not look at customers – just as our thinking does not look at finance and accounting, production and quality management. As such, many business concepts by design overlooked customers and never claimed to look at them either. Customers were part of the environment, somewhere out there. Just like this book gently looks past the accounting, production and finance departments, among others, except for delivering a common language and knowledge-sharing platform.

For those concepts related to strategy, marketing and sales, the reason for overlooking customers is different: Because the concepts did not solve the segmentation problem, focus was put on contributing with other insights according to the executive requirements of context, accountability and result. The valuable contributions, thus, focused on resource efficiency, not market efficiency.

In a nutshell, all concepts made customers and focus on customers important, at least as a sideline comment. But none of the concepts made customer insight operational. CUBEical Thinking offers this operational use of customer knowledge by turning tacit knowledge into explicit knowledge and knowledge into action. On top of the valuable pieces already supplied, CUBEical Thinking delivers a central piece – customer knowledge. The missing piece pictures the customer universes in which the firm competes for the hearts and wallets of the customers.

In most developed economies, marketing and sales expenditures including salaries account for at least 15% of GDP. Every percent which can be converted from being non-productive into being productive and targeted toward profitable customers will end up directly on the bottom line as increased EBITDA. CUBEical Thinking offers a central piece for the EBITDA puzzle. It does not replace other views, it connects them. It does not question their founding logic, it helps to sharpen their customer view and the integration of customer knowledge. Hereby, EBITDA can be truly optimized by balancing internal efficiency against market efficiency.

From CUBEical Thinking to shareholder value

In Chapter 2, we started out by looking at the executive agenda of driving profitable revenue growth. In our search for solving some business challenges, we developed the CUBEical Thinking framework. Now it is time to make a final test – and relate the framework back to the executive agenda. In order to have a "real" test, one should use a different line of arguments – anything else is a backward step leading to where we started.

For that purpose, we look at shareholder value as this is also on the executive agenda. Of course, shareholder value is tightly connected to EBITDA. But the common model for shareholder value discussions is not the financial-driven EBITDA equation but a capital model. As illustrated in Figure 9.4, the market value of the firm and thus the return to shareholders stems from two sources, the financial capital and the intellectual capital of the firm. The intellectual capital

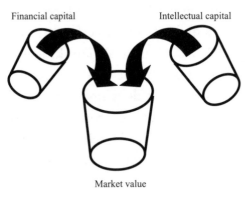

Financial capital   Intellectual capital

Market value

Figure 9.4 Market valuation of the firm.

represents the value of the knowledge held by the firm and its employees.

Referring back to the discussion of knowledge management, it is of crucial importance to shareholders that the tacit knowledge represented by the employees' capabilities and competencies is made explicit and structured into an organizational framework and supporting business processes. If not, a significant part of the market value of the firm is influenced by turnover of employees.

Customer knowledge is only seen as intellectual capital when this knowledge is employed for driving up- and cross-selling and for driving new product development and innovation. Improvements in selling method and accelerating up- and cross-selling increase a firm's customer value. There is more money in each customer. This value increase is based on the CRM system supporting up- and cross-selling. With the increased understanding, the platform for innovation and operation is established. Thus, the CUBEical Thinking framework supports market value and returns to shareholders and is, therefore, of interest to executives. There is a clear connection between the framework and the executive agenda.

Profitable, two-digit, top-line growth rates make sense to shareholders especially when knowing that results are obtained by design and not by accident. CUBEical Thinking addresses a fundamental challenge of all firms to manage and leverage upon the human capital, the tacit knowledge held by the customer-facing employees of the firm, by making it explicit and thereby accessible and proprietary to the firm.

Profitable revenue growth is achieved through creating truly loyal customers. Due to the strong connection of strategy and implementation, analysts trust in firms' executives ability to succeed in realizing profitable growth.

10

The fast moving consumer goods universe

C UBEical Thinking applies to firms operating in B2B as well as in B2C business environments. Focusing on B2B firms, the environment is often much larger than its immediate customers. If not selling to consumers, a firm's customers have customers themselves. A firm's customers have, of course, to be concerned about their customers. It is their responsibility to understand and activate their customers' universes.

Often, customers demand that their suppliers also understand their customers. And selling gets a lot easier when a supplier has not only understood the immediate customer's needs but also how these needs derive from the customer's interactions with its own customers. This is particularly true for fast moving consumer goods (FMCG) firms because they need to address both end users and intermediaries, e.g. retail and convenience channels (off-trade) as well as hotel, restaurant, cafés, etc. (on-trade).

When distribution chains do not function, no one along the chain earns money. Thus, the customer universes of the intermediaries and of the end users must be aligned. Therefore, an understanding of one market universe is not enough; the understanding must be enlarged to two layers and the interrelations between different market universes must be explored. In this chapter we show how two different layers of the value chain, the FMCG intermediary and the FMCG end user, can be addressed by using the CUBEical framework.

FMCG set-up

To a large extent, fast moving consumer goods are distributed by retailers. Consumers cannot buy Coca-Cola from the Coca-Cola Company, Frosties and Coco Pops from Kelloggs, or a draft beer from Carlsberg. Most of the private shopping takes place in supermarkets. Most of the supermarkets are part of retail chains. WalMart, one of the world's largest firms, is a retail chain. So retailing is big business, and so is manufacturing of fast moving consumer goods, by firms like Procter and Gamble, Unilever, Nestlé, Masterfoods and all those other well-known firms.

Each of the two layers has two different perspectives. An end user is not only consuming but also buying the goods. These two processes need to be separated, thus there is a consumer and a shopper. Likewise, the intermediary is not only selling to shoppers but also buying from the FMCG manufacturers. These two activities are often performed at different levels in the organization and it has proven valuable to distinguish

Figure 10.1 The FMCG–retailer–consumer chain.

between the channel partner (the buying side of retailing) and the retailer (the selling side of retailing). Thus, there are four perspectives to keep track of (Figure 10.1).

In a nutshell, FMCG firms have key account managers for handling the intermediary's headquarters and for constantly activating the account. The FMCG firms also have sales people who visit the shops of the intermediaries to, talk with the shop managers, furbish the shop with in-store equipment and refill shelves, among many other things. Of course, the specific division of labor between the FMCG firm and the intermediary is subject to the individual contract. But apart from some specifics, the set-up is similar (Figure 10.1).

All of the FMCG firms are masters of branding, at least they use a lot of money for mass communication. They also buy a lot of market research about shoppers and consumers. In addition, they fully employ key account management. FMCG is an industry which must intensively work with all four perspectives to make end users buy.

The ultimate achievement of the FMCG manufacturer is:

- To catch the attention of the consumer;

- To trigger the interest of the consumer;

- To have the consumer show desire by going to the retailer where the good can be purchased (i.e. to become a shopper);

- To have the shopper take action by picking the good and taking it to the cashier to pay for it.

It is the same AIDA process but the four perspectives makes it complex (Figure 10.2). Within FMCG firms, the different steps in the AIDA process are often handled by different departments sitting in functional silos within the FMCG manufactures' organizations. Typically, each of the functional

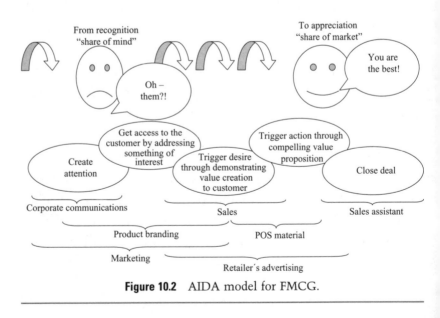

Figure 10.2 AIDA model for FMCG.

silos runs "their" business with "their" segmentation framework.

The sales departments on their side are working with the intermediaries as their prime customer. Sales people know that intermediaries differ and that they consequently should be served differently, but as nobody else is requesting these insights intermediaries are not segmented. Instead, sales departments take the position that the better they are at advising the intermediary on how to drive the category, the more influence sales people will get on how the intermediary runs the business. As sales people often argue, as long as the category grows the FMCG manufacturers will get their fair share. For sales people, the intermediary and not the consumer has the prime focus.

In addition to sales, the FMCG manufacturer communicates to customers in parallel with the intermediary. Often the intermediaries' marketing budget is handsomely funded by the FMCG manufacturers' trade promotion funds. Furthermore, to close the AIDA process, the intermediaries' and FMCG firms' in-store personnel can also influence the buying decision of shoppers and consumers.

Recent trends in FMCG firms are:

- A stronger consumer branding focus on occasions and situations: After realizing that demographical segmentation did not work, the focus is currently on situational consumption. As discussed in Chapter 3, these situational approaches have delivered long lists of situations which cut across product management lines – a source of confusion. Product branding is often linked to occasions but due to inadequate segmentation it most often misses the target. The occasion being addressed is typically selected by taking the number of consumers who, based on gender, age and other demographic data, might have an interest in the occasion and thereby potentially could have an interest in the product in question. Often the selection of the occasion is not based on a segmentation framework but on the advice of the FMCG manufacturer's media and advertising agencies or on input from the research companies helping the FMCG manufacturer to keep track of shoppers and consumers.

- A stronger focus on shoppers: After realizing that a number of decisions are made in the shop due to low consumer branding effectiveness, FMCG firms are looking into shopper behavior. Firms have developed long lists with different shopping situations. They focus also on how shopper buying decisions can be influenced through advertising and in-store communications. Hereby, marketing is seeking ways of guiding the sales departments' in-store activities, for example space and category management, and the use of point-of-sales (POS) material and in-store furniture.

From the above it is evident that a common language for turning all the tacit knowledge about end users and intermediaries into explicit knowledge would help FMCG manufacturers and intermediaries to improve their efficiency and their results. In the following, we unfold a CUBEical model for FMCG. We start with consumers and shoppers, i.e. the B2C part of the business.

Consumer and shopper universes

FMCG manufacturers know that end users differ and consequently by applying CUBEical segmentation, consumers and shoppers can be segmented according to their behaviors and ways of making decisions. Thus, end user types can be developed. There are consumers who are really interested in the product category, reading all product tests, knowing the history of all manufacturers and where they buy their materials. Logically, the end user type is the same regardless of whether the end user is consuming or shopping.

What differs is the situation. Therefore, end user segmentation is split up into two cubes. A consumer cube covering consumer situations in which the goods are consumed and a shopper cube covering the situations in which shopping takes place (Figure 10.3).

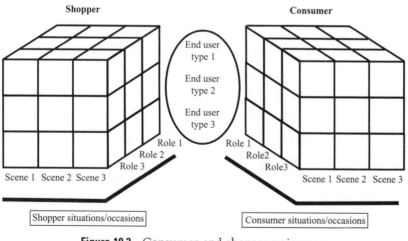

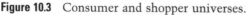

Figure 10.3 Consumer and shopper universes.

The consumer situations are split up into roles and scenes. Roles typically describe the social context in which consumption takes place, i.e. with friends, alone, with family, with spouse, etc., while the scene describes the physical location where the consumption takes place, i.e. at home, in a cinema, in a hotel room, in a garden, etc. A typical situation for FMCG goods is watching TV at home with friends. In this situation, different end user types demand different products.

Thus, by entering the competitive arenas associated with a given end user type, consumer needs can be revealed and opportunities for setting consumer expectations beyond the reach of competition can be documented in the consumer opportunity map. Thus, the framework fully applies for FMCG manufactures to gain insight into the consumer universes and to take market leadership by setting and fulfilling consumer expectations beyond the reach of competition. The dimensions typically considered are different products, different package size and different bundling opportunities as supplementary products associated with the occasion vary.

The same applies to end users as shoppers. The shopper situations are split up into roles and scenes. Roles typically describe the type of shopping, e.g. one product shopping (the one the person forgot last time), cherry picking (just going for special products or temporary offerings), major weekly shopping (the long shopping list covering many categories) while scenes describe the physical location where the shopper expects to pick the goods, i.e. the physical location within a store (e.g. entrance area, kiosk, beverages department, fruit and greens department, non-food department).

Thus, the end user type in combination with the individual shopping situations guides the FMCG manufacturer to the different physical locations within the premises of the retailer. Also, it guides the FMCG manufacturer as to which products should be positioned where and on how the products should be exposed, packaged and priced to fulfill the expectations and needs of the shopper beyond the reach of the competition.

In line with the framework, a shopper opportunity map can be established. Based on this, a shopper strategy map can be developed to pin down the guidelines for implementation.

Channel partner and retailer universes

Regarding the intermediaries, FMCG manufacturers describe them as different. Consequently, intermediaries can be segmented according to their behaviors and ways of making decisions. By performing this segmentation, the intermediary represents two different perspectives, the channel partner towards the FMCG and the retailer (the shop) towards the consumer. Thus, on the one hand, the FMCG manufacturer meets the intermediary as the buyer of goods. On the other hand, the FMCG manufacturer meets the very same intermediary showing the very same behaviors and ways of making decisions but now as a seller of the FMCG manufacturer's goods in its shop (Figure 10.4).

Therefore segmentation is split up into a channel partner segmentation covering the buyer situations where the business between the intermediary as channel partner and the

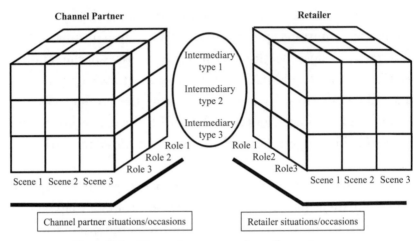

Figure 10.4 Channel partner and retailer universes.

FMCG manufacturer is performed. The second cube, the retailer cube, covers the intermediary as retailer when planning and executing sales in the shops together with the sales people of the FMCG manufacturer.

The channel partner situations are split up into roles and scenes. Roles typically describe the functional position of the representatives of the channel partner when interacting with the FMCG manufacturer, i.e. procurement manager, warehouse manager, logistics manager, etc. Scenes are typically meeting rooms, offices, warehouse facilities etc. at the channel partner or the FMCG manufacturer.

For retailer situations in the retailer cube the roles are functional positions of the persons performing the operational in-store tasks required to drive sales, i.e. refilling shelves, putting up POS materials, installing in-store furniture, etc. The scenes in the retailer cube describe the physical location where the goods are expected to be picked, i.e. the physical location within a store – entrance area, kiosk, beverages department, fruit and greens department, non-food department.

Again, opportunities can be identified regarding the business between the retailer and the FMCG manufacturer and likewise business opportunities can be identified regarding the way the retailer and the FMCG manufacturer together are pushing the category in question. The strategy maps for the channel partner and for the retailer guide business development and implementation.

Based on the insights provided by the shopper segmentation, the FMCG manufacturer can now advise the retailers on how to improve their results by better addressing shoppers.

Connecting the universes

While it is behaviors and the way of making decisions of the end users which connect the consumer and the shopper cubes and while it is behaviors and decision-making patterns of intermediaries which connect the channel partner and the retailer cubes, it is the scenes of the shopper and the retailer cube which connect shoppers and retailers. In their efforts to sell goods in their shops, retailers furbish their shops in order to make shoppers buy. The retailer and the shopper meet at the same scene. With this connection in place, FMCG firms are provided with a market model which is connected end to end. The model takes into consideration the four very different perspectives and real behavior of end users and intermediaries (Figure 10.5).

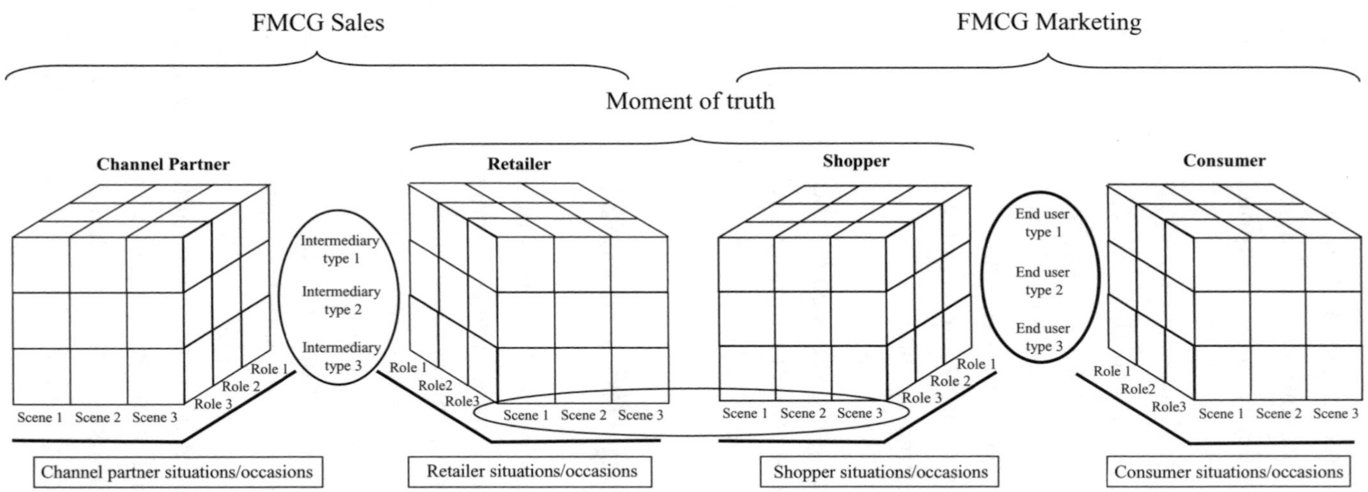

FMCG Sales

Moment of truth

FMCG Marketing

Channel Partner

Scene 1 Scene 2 Scene 3

Role 1
Role 2
Role 3

Channel partner situations/occasions

Intermediary type 1
Intermediary type 2
Intermediary type 3

Retailer

Role 1
Role2
Role3

Scene 1 Scene 2 Scene 3

Retailer situations/occasions

Shopper

Role 1
Role 2
Role 3

Scene 1 Scene 2 Scene 3

Shopper situations/occasions

End user type 1
End user type 2
End user type 3

Consumer

Role 1
Role2
Role3

Scene 1 Scene 2 Scene 3

Consumer situations/occasions

Figure 10.5 CUBEical Thinking for FMCG manufacturers.

Hereby, CUBEical Thinking for FMCG manufacturers is driving relationships with end users and intermediaries by linking segmentation, strategy and implementation into a cohesive, consistent, easily understandable and easily implemented business framework (Figure 10.6). The consumer shopper framework reveals the needs and expectations of the consumer as to consumption and shopping. Typically, these universes form the foundation for marketing's work on branding, brand positioning and consumer communications.

To do the shopping the shopper needs to select a retailer, a shop to go to. Depending on the end user type and shopping situation, the shopper selects a retailer where the wanted goods can be purchased. Through shopper communications, marketing will try to take the shopper as far as possible through the AIDA process to ensure that the shopper goes to the retailer which best suits the shopping situation pinned down in the shopper strategy map.

While the shopper framework provides insights into the needs and expectations of the shopper, the retailer framework provides insight into what the various retailers potentially can offer. Retailers try attracting shoppers to their shop. In this context, based on the insights into the shopper universe provided by marketing, sales people can advise the retailer on how to target shopper communications. Likewise, based on the shopper strategy map, sales people can translate the shopper requirements into the retailer strategy map pinning down how sales people in cooperation with the retailer in question can perform the required in-store activities to set and fulfill the shopper's expectations beyond the reach of competition. Hence, by comparing the two the FMCG

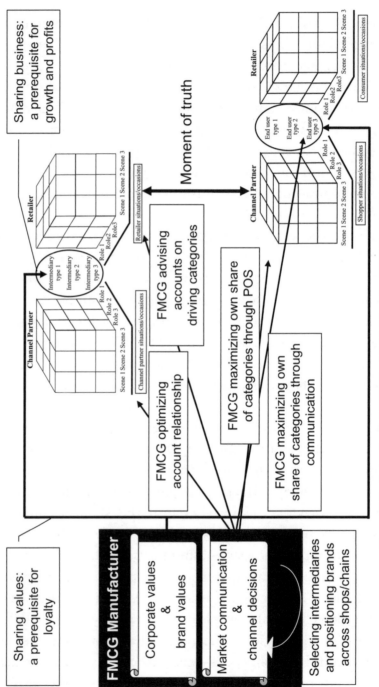

Figure 10.6 Overview of CUBEical Thinking for FMCG manufacturers.

manufacturer can select channel partners and place products and brands within retailers to fulfill the needs and expectations of the shoppers.

Managing retailers is in the hands of the FMCG sales people in cooperation with the employees of the retailer. In developing the retail strategy map sales, marketing and the representatives of the retailer have to work closely together to maximize and balance the resource efficiency and the market efficiency of the activities performed to drive sales of the FMCG manufacturer's goods. Furthermore, it is in the hands of sales to drive the business with the channel partner. In doing so it is sales' responsibility to secure the overall profitability of serving consumers through intermediaries.

Summing up CUBEical Thinking in FMCG

In this chapter we outlined how CUBEical Thinking applies to situations where the firm is selling through intermediaries and thus has to manage two interrelated businesses. As an example, we picked the FMCG industry which, from our experience, is representing vast opportunities for increasing market efficiency and thereby for making idle marketing investments productive.

CUBEical Thinking for FMCG provides FMCG manufacturers with a transparent, consistent and easy-to-understand framework bringing insight into the dynamics between brands, communication channels and consumers. This is in contrast with the highly fragmented and non-transparent way FMCG business is performed today. From our experience FMCG manufacturers have all the knowledge required to implement and benefit from the CUBEical Thinking framework. Thus, the CUBEical Thinking framework itself provides the structure for turning the tacit knowledge into explicit knowledge which can be structured, shared and leveraged upon. When introducing CUBEical Thinking FMCG manufacturers will realize how most of the analysis provided by research firms can be turned into creating significant value when being modified to and interpreted within the four different cubes.

11

The key account management universe

UNTIL NOW WE HAVE TREATED A CUSTOMER AS ONE customer. We segmented firms as firms and individuals as individuals. While this makes a lot of sense, reality is sometimes a bit more complex – at least customer-facing people see a more varied picture than one customer. A typical comment is: "The customer I am dealing with is highly complex and there are many people involved in the relationship. I do not feel that all of them are within one customer type."

So there are customers within a customer – not only various customers distributed along the value chain as discussed in the previous chapter. This customers-in-a-customer phenomenon is not a rare exemption from the rule. Actually, most of the interactions in markets are influenced by a number of people, thus decisions are the result of various persons each potentially with their own requirements. Once multi-person decision-making is detected, firms need to consider the people involved as one account because they make a joint purchasing decision. It makes little sense to segment all involved people differently and to put them in different segmentation models because a firm either wins or loses the whole account. In order to gain an integrated view of the customer, firms need an integrated model to deal with accounts. As such situations are normally associated with key account management in practice, we also use the term here.

In this chapter, we explain how CUBEical Thinking handles this challenge and aids with structuring of multi-person inter-actions. We use a B2B key account situation as the background for explaining our thinking. Nevertheless, the arguments are as valid for B2C multi-person situations: Car and house purchases, holiday decisions, etc.

In order to solve the multi-person challenge, we must first get an overview of who the customer is.

Who is the customer?

Regardless of the segmentation framework used, a central question must be answered: Who is the customer? As explored in Chapter 10, various customers can be found along the value chain. It is important to find out who should be regarded as customers. And whom to call customer. At a meeting with a newspaper publisher, discussions went strangely until we realized that the term customer is used for advertisers as they are basically paying the big amounts and are of major importance for profits. Those buying the newspaper are called readers. Many industries and firms have their own

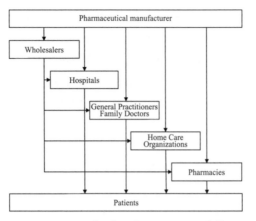

Figure 11.1 Customer network of a pharmaceutical firm's value chain.

definitions. Pharmaceuticals face plenty of potential decision makers and thereby potential customers along their value chain (Figure 11.1): Patients, doctors, hospitals, etc. We highly recommend that firms draw a map of their customer network and attach intuitively understandable terms to the different types of customers. If not, different departments will talk forever with each other about customers but never understand whom they are actually referring to.

All of these layers of customers need their own segmentation. At first sight this sounds rather complex and, thus, some managers would rather ignore complexity and keep it simple. But if a business is complex, treating it as simple is potentially suboptimal, to say the least. The better option is to use the CUBEical framework to capture the complexity and describe it in intuitive, stable and efficient terms. Hereby the different customer layers can be connected, just as we explained in Chapter 10 for FMCG manufacturers. These connections reduce complexity a great deal and actually map out the inner logic of the value chain.

Once the value chain is mapped out, focus can shift to a single customer layer. Let's take hospitals from the above example; who does the firm meet in hospitals? While treating a hospital as one customer is an intriguing idea, in reality things are different. Within a given hospital the pharmaceutical firm has contacts with:

- Various doctors in various departments;

- Various nurses in various departments;

- Various people in the purchasing department;

- Various people within the hospital management team.

So there are plenty of potential customers within the customer, the hospital. When segmenting individuals, this problem does not exist. Ambiguity about the customer can only exist when segmentation is performed at an aggregation level where customers are represented by two or more individuals involved in making a decision, i.e. where a firm deals with an account. In cases where different individuals of one customer make decisions independently from each other, we are back at segmenting individuals. This is typically the case with decentralized purchasing in large corporations where different business units are the relevant segmentation level.

A word of caution before we continue: If ambiguity as to who the customer is within the customer cannot be solved, the customer relationship will not last long because no firm can satisfy the unknown. If the ambiguity is deliberately engineered by the customer, the firm should not invest in the relationship. But we have heard the occasional comment from managers, especially from large firms: "If you find out how my firm operates and who makes the decisions, would you please tell me." What is meant as a joke is actually good advice. If the ambiguity is not engineered but a feature of the customer organization, the firm should assist the customer in aligning business processes and dissolve the ambiguity. This strengthens business relationship in two ways: It makes it easier, actually possible, to manage the relationship and the customer is thankful for the support in solving a problem.

Let's continue our hospital example. The hospital is in the process of selecting a pharmaceutical supplier for wound bandages which are used widely across departments. As the decision is made for the whole hospital, the hospital is the relevant unit of analysis, the hospital is the account. As described, there are many potential customers within the customer and the challenge is to segment the hospital correctly. There are three possible account scenarios: Centralized accounts, aligned accounts and fragmented accounts.

Centralized accounts

The centralized model is rather simple because the account basically can be considered as one decision maker who decides on behalf of other members of the organization. As such, segmentation is back to focusing on one person.

Of course, it is nice to know the many other people at the hospital, but it is has no direct impact on selling because the decision is made by another person. Even though it doesn't make sense to try to influence the users as they have no direct influence on supplier selection, it is important to understand the situations and occasions the users are in to advise the central purchaser. Actually, purchasers are doing their best to fulfill the needs and expectations of the members of the organization they are working for – at least they should be. Sometimes these needs are just not made explicit. By looking at the competitive arenas making up the purchaser's internal market, the firm can provide the purchaser with insight which can have great business impact for the relationship with the centralized account. With centralized accounts, resource efficiency can be increased by reducing contact to non-decision makers in numbers (how many) or in intensity (how often).

While there are many centralized accounts, other accounts are truly represented by different people who jointly make a decision – as we discuss in the following.

Aligned accounts

When applying key account management, the customer representatives across the customer's organization are treated individually by the firm's customer-facing employees. But is differentiation necessary when employees should behave similarly according to the customer's corporate values?

For the sake of the argument, let's assume the customer has a strong corporate culture which ensures that employees mirror the customer's values and beliefs in their behavior and way of decision-making. Hereby, the employees are aligned with the strategy of the firm they represent. Even in these cases, customer representatives do have different requirements. Our work identifies two reasons for this: Different responsibilities within the customer firm and different personalities.

Different responsibilities

People in firms have different requirements because they have different responsibilities. These different responsibilities are normally attached to their positions in firms, i.e. their role. A purchaser is concerned about the contract and product delivery, the production manager is concerned about maintenance procedures, the sales and marketing people think of implications for their customers, the CEO reflects on EBITDA implications, and so forth; so different people have different thoughts on their minds. Continuing the hospital example, the purchaser may ask about just-in-time delivery and payment conditions, the doctor is concerned about the healing process, the nurse about handling the bandage, and the director thinks of liability risks and overall costs of treatment.

These differences in requirements have been described as buying center roles – and this is what they are: Different roles. Typically, when developing the customer activity chart (Chapter 5), the different people are connected to different roles and often they appear in different scenes. In this case CUBEical segmentation handles the complexity by assigning the decision makers to roles. As such, the only difference from the "normal" model is that the different roles of a

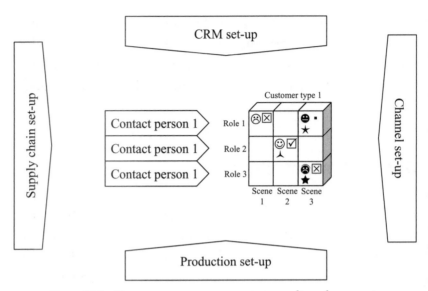

Figure 11.2   Key account management at an aligned account.

customer (the hospital) are performed by different people. Thus, the notion of competitive arenas remains unchanged.

Figure 11.2 illustrates the key account management model with different people involved. As assumed above, the hospital is represented by only one customer type because all employees behave the same based on a strong impact of corporate values and beliefs. This is why we call this type of account "aligned" – all employees think and act in line with the overall strategy of the firm but the firm meets them in their specific combination of roles and scenes.

Personality

The differences in people's behavior are also influenced by personality, i.e. personal preferences as to behaviors and decision-making patterns. People are extroverts or intro-verts, some are assertive and others not, some are interested in power, some hate responsibility. Some control every detail and others think more in meters than in millimeters. Yes, people are different and these personal differences are observable in interactions. As such, a wave of personality tests is washing through sales and purchasing departments to identify these differences. Prospective firms have even organized their sales people's allocation to accounts according to personality tests, so the profile of the key account manager matches the profile of the counterpart at the customer.

While it makes perfect sense to optimize negotiation results and relationship atmosphere, and actually has the advantage of driving profitable revenue growth even further, it makes little sense when discussing product portfolios with regard to up- and cross-selling. Based on product features why should the extravert doctor prefer a wound bandage different to the one preferred by an introvert doctor?

The wave of personality testing makes key account managers focus on individual personality differences rather than on business similarities. So instead of driving up- and cross-selling, managers are busy optimizing interpersonal atmospheric turbulences. At the end of the personality process, two perfectly matched persons can express their disappointment in the mutual understanding that this meeting was meaningless because the seller did not know the customer universe and thus was left with product feature selling. So the order of increasing sophistication should first take a business perspective and then the personality one. If someone comes up with a good business proposal, i.e. a relevant offering solving a customer's needs, the customer representative is normally extremely professional and survives any possible personality differences. And by the way: Coping with different people is what sales people are good at.

Our experience is that behaviors and ways of making decisions of many accounts are well aligned with the customer type of the firm they represent. For these firms, the role dimension and thereby the notion of competitive arenas solves the ambiguity. If there is still ambiguity about customer representatives' behavior, individuals of the customer do not behave and make decisions in line with the behaviors and ways of making decisions of the customer type. Thus, the above assumption of strong corporate values and beliefs is not always true. As this situation is not as uncommon as many executives hope for, we explore the implications of key accounts being misaligned regarding their behaviors and ways of making decisions in the following. We call these "fragmented accounts".

Fragmented accounts

If individuals representing a key account behave and make decisions each in their own way and if these behaviors and ways of making decisions are out of line with those described for the customer type in question, the customer's business is in disarray. Given that the different customer types in the market universe cover this possible variation, the different individuals behave as different customer types (Figure 11.3). The situation in the figure shows a firm with no common

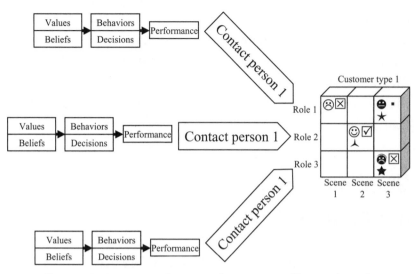

Figure 11.3   Fragmented account being internally misaligned.

strategy and with corporate values – if any – not being anchored across the organization.

Given that different customer types demand different offerings, it is impossible for a firm to satisfy the above illustrated customer. Satisfying the needs of one individual will automatically dissatisfy another. Therefore, this customer should be a non-customer. Or as sales people often point out: "Life is too short to work with such customers." There are more attractive customers around.

Fragmented customers are often large corporations where "the left hand does not know what the right hand is doing". Being in the potential key account management league with regards to potential sales volume, firms are spending fortunes on building business with such customers without realizing the chaotic way these customers run their businesses. Without insights into customer types and thus identification of the problem, all investments will be in vain. The only way to work with such customers is to develop the customer organization in order to align them – or to stop dealing with them.

Summing up key account management

CUBEical Thinking is also applicable to key account management. In fact, it actually supports key account management by bringing clarity to account mapping in terms of roles. Furthermore, the framework potentially strengthens the relationships with centralized accounts as the firm can provide the contact person with a deeper understanding of the needs and expectations of the organization through insights into the competitive arenas. Likewise for the aligned accounts the deep understanding of an account provided through the customer type of the account and the roles and scenes of the employees helps in driving business. Finally, the framework enables identification of fragmented accounts in which meaningless investments should be avoided.

12

The merger and acquisition universe

THROUGHOUT THE BOOK SO FAR, WE HAVE FOCUSED ON organic growth. With an increased understanding of customers, firms are able to profitably grow their business. Growing the firm organically by making customers the pivotal focus on the executive agenda is the basic growth path of all firms. But organic growth is not the only way forward. Given fierce competition in local, regional and global markets, firms also look for growth opportunities based on mergers and acquisitions.

Huge amounts of money are offered for firms with limited bearing in the book value or in its financial and intellectual capital. The mantra for explaining the bidding sum is the effect on EBITDA when realizing potential synergies. But what looks good in a strategy plan and the merger and acquisition press release, often causes headaches during implementation. For some firms this headache develops into a nightmare.

Despite the perceived potential synergies prior to a merger or acquisition, synergies seldom materialize and deliver the expected EBITDA growth in the post-merger phase because the traditional inward-looking business focus of many corporations tends to neglect customers as the pivotal focus of business. Not considering the impact of mergers and acquisitions on customers disconnects the strategy from EBITDA growth. The inward-looking focus mirrors the traditional due diligence processes tending to put more focus on financial and legal matters and less on verifying how the expected synergies can be harvested from the customer and market side.

In relation to mergers and acquisitions, CUBEical Thinking has proven to facilitate the process of finding the right match between firms and, subsequently, realizing the integration efficiently. In this chapter, we discuss how CUBEical Thinking improves evaluating the potential synergies of integrating firms, and realizing the EBITDA growth when implementing the integration of firms in question. We illustrate how CUBEical Thinking assists with avoiding the merger and acquisition headaches by ensuring fit and synergy realization. Thus, CUBEical Thinking is both a framework for increasing pre-merger and acquisition analysis quality and post-merger and acquisition integration quality.

Alignment of business processes

In order to discuss the challenges of mergers and acquisitions in more detail, we need to consider the alignment of the existing business processes across the business units of the firm in question. To facilitate the reading of the chapter, we refer to the existing firm as the acquiring firm and the new unit being integrated through the merger or acquisition as the acquired firm – even though mergers presume an equal standing of the two.

Up to this point in the book, we have discussed a customer as one customer and a firm as one firm. In Chapter 11 we extended this view to customers with different functions. This discussion has led to a distinction of different accounts and the notion of account management. But it is not only customers who have different functions and units, firms are also organized into business units, regions, divisions, etc. Very often, firms have a corporate headquarters, a regional structure (typically US, Americas, Europe, Far and Middle East, Africa, rest of world) and local business units referring to these (Figure 12.1). Here we can also distinguish between centralized, aligned and fragmented firms.

There are two fundamentally different ways of organizing business units within a corporation. One, all business units

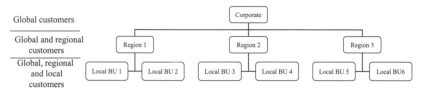

Figure 12.1 Corporate structure and different customers.

are similar and have different regions as their domain. Here alignment deals with best practice and standardization issues. The aim in this case is to share best practice across the organization. Two, all business units have their own competence field. Alignment deals with making the individual units' competence available across the organization. The aim in this situation is to leverage competences across the organization. In any case, and in all variations of the two ways of organizing business units within a corporation, there is a need for alignment of business processes to realize synergies.

Just as we discussed with key account management in Chapter 11, firms can be centralized, aligned or fragmented in their operations of existing business units before a merger and acquisition takes place. The existing alignment is a measure of the achieved synergies within the existing corporate structure – low alignment means little leverage between business units and limited utilization of synergies; and high alignment implies realization of synergies. Thus, a low degree of alignment typically implies that mergers and acquisitions will only add to the problems the acquiring firm is already encountering in making its business profitable. At least such mergers and acquisitions are unlikely to result in synergies, as realizing synergies is not a core competence of low alignment firms.

Alignment of corporate structures cannot be assumed as a given, even though the objective of maximizing EBITDA growth is also driven by identifying and exercising synergies – thus, fitting the executive agenda. Therefore, before discussing the various scenarios for mergers and acquisitions it is

Figure 12.2   Business process as a source of synergies.

worthwhile looking into the mechanisms and complexity of aligning global organizations.

Business processes often span global, regional and local business environments. Therefore business processes, outlined in Figure 12.2, are designed and managed at global, regional or local levels. These different levels do not always follow the same key success factors – in fact, they often compete with and contradict each other. This is the challenge of alignment.

Whatever the design logic may be, business processes have a direct influence on the local business unit's behavior vis-à-vis its customers. In a nutshell, all business is local to the extent that all business is based on interaction. As such, there is a direct link between business processes, global alignment and customer loyalty, as explained in Chapter 7. By aligning business processes at global or regional levels across the business units of a firm, the ways of behaving in competitive arenas change. Consequently, customers, as well as customer-facing employees, often feel that alignment changes are made for no obvious reasons and without any positive impact.

From our experience in dealing with business processes alignment, the concept of minimum global and regional requirements has proven to be an efficient way of realizing synergies while allowing adaptation to local markets. We use the terms *global minimum requirements* and *regional minimum requirements* to refer to the global and regional business process which a local business unit shall be able to perform to service the firm's global and regional customers and/or to fulfill the requirements of corporate controlling. In addition to these global and regional minimum requirements, the local business units can design their business processes to suit the local requirements of their local customers.

As global customers must be dealt with globally, regionally and locally, and as regional customers can be dealt with regionally and locally (and all three levels of global, regional and local customers are served within one firm), synergies depend on a common segmentation framework, as well as a common structure for grouping goods and services.

As discussed earlier, the general picture is that few firms have good segmentation frameworks and, to make things even worse, different organizational levels within firms operate with different segmentation frameworks across the organization. This mirrors the situation described for FMCG firms where different functions have different segmentation frameworks. The situation is often driven by subsequent mergers and acquisitions over time where no effort was made during integration to align the different frameworks of the different business units. In addition, ambiguity exists as to at which level of detail customer segmentation should be performed – typically for demo-firmo-graphics. Interestingly, this ambiguity is core to the local business units' resistance to change the way they are driving their businesses. Typically, local business units who have been spreading themselves thinly across an industry will argue for a high aggregation level in order to present revenues of a size which could imply that their local business is profitable. In contrast, business units who have penetrated an industry will typically argue for a more detailed level of segmentation as they already have structured their local business accordingly. Likewise, business units who have substantial sales of related products will argue for a detailed structure for product groups, while other business units with less sales will argue for a more coarse structure.

Therefore, aligning a global firm and thus rationalizing and targeting customer and product portfolios at local, regional and global level requires good segmentation practice. Only by following the criteria of good customer segmentation, can synergies across business units be identified and harvested through focusing resources on the global, regional and local customers whose customer universes fit the competencies and offerings of the global, regional and local levels of the organization.

In laying the strategy for how to align the corporation and thereby deciding on where and how to compete, the firm has to employ the global, regional and local profitability matrix as outlined in Figure 12.3.

Global

Customer type \ Product group	PG 1	PG 2	PG 3	PG 4
Customer type 1	$/ROI	$/ROI	$/ROI	$/ROI
Customer type 2	$/ROI	$/ROI	$/ROI	$/ROI

Regional

Customer type \ Product group	PG 1	PG 2	PG 3	PG 4	PG 5	PG 6
Customer type 1	$/ROI	$/ROI	$/ROI	$/ROI	$/ROI	$/ROI
Customer type 2	$/ROI	$/ROI	$/ROI	$/ROI	$/ROI	$/ROI
Customer type 3	$/ROI	$/ROI	$/ROI	$/ROI	$/ROI	$/ROI

Local

Customer type \ Product group	PG 1	PG 2	PG 3	PG 4	PG 5	PG 6	PG 7
Customer type 1	$/ROI	$/ROI	$/ROI	$/ROI	$/ROI	$/ROI	$/ROI
Customer type 2	$/ROI	$/ROI	$/ROI	$/ROI	$/ROI	$/ROI	$/ROI
Customer type 3	$/ROI	$/ROI	$/ROI	$/ROI	$/ROI	$/ROI	$/ROI
Customer type 4	$/ROI	$/ROI	$/ROI	$/ROI	$/ROI	$/ROI	$/ROI
Customer type 5	$/ROI	$/ROI	$/ROI	$/ROI	$/ROI	$/ROI	$/ROI

Figure 12.3 Customer and product portfolios at global, regional and local level.

Only when the aggregation of actual and potential revenues and profits being filled into the cells in Figure 12.3 rests on good customer segmentation, can a firm truly align its operations across its business units. If not, the segments are not mirroring how business with customers is really performed and products are aggregated into groups with no connection to reality. The picture of who to serve with which goods and services changes completely across different aggregation levels.

In aligning a firm across its business units, the aim is to decide globally, regionally and locally on which customers to serve with which products in order to secure profitable revenue growth through exercising potential synergies. Typically, there are global customers who are only being served in some regions and global customers for whom the market penetration is higher in some regions than in others. Consequently, the aim is to identify and plan up- and cross-sales opportunities based on the knowledge gained across regions; again highlighting the need for a common segmentation framework. Likewise, regional customers may be served successfully by some business units, while this is not the case with other business units. Consequently, the corporate headquarters will be looking for opportunities to leverage the knowledge on how to serve regional customers across business units. Furthermore, business units have local customers and the best practice of serving these is also an opportunity for leveraging knowledge. Therefore, returning to the concept of minimum global and regional requirements, the use of customer types across all levels of the organization provides the vehicle to create transparency and consistency in pursuing global, regional and local business opportunities.

Scenarios for mergers and acquisitions

Based on the above, assuming that the firm has been aligned prior to a merger or acquisition, let's look into some scenarios for these. In discussing mergers and acquisitions it is worthwhile distinguishing between four basic scenarios (Figure 12.4).

Foundation			Promise		Delivery	
Firm Types	Roles	Scenes	Competence	Offering	Fulfillment	Performance

Scenario 1: Financial mergers and acquisitions The corporate firm is spreading risk and/or pursuing an up-side through investing in a number of different industries representing different business cycles.

The acquired firm has a different strategy and is serving different customer universes than those of other business units belonging to the corporate firm.		The acquired firm has unrelated competencies and offerings than those of the other business units belonging to the corporate firm.		The acquired firm is serving unrelated customer universes than those of the other business units belonging to the corporate firm.

Scenario 2: Penetration Mergers and Acquisitions The corporate firm is pursuing market share.

The acquired firm has a similar strategy and is serving similar customer universes as those of other business units belonging to the corporate firm.		The acquired firm has similar competencies and offerings as those of the other business units belonging to the corporate firm.		The acquired firm is serving similar customer universes as those of the other business units belonging to the corporate firm.

Scenario 3: Internationalization Mergers and Acquisitions The corporate firm is pursuing production capacity in local market in order to serve regional and global customers.

The acquired firm has a local scope and is serving similar local customer universes as those of other business units belonging to the corporate firm.		The acquired firm has similar production competencies as those of the other business units belonging to the corporate firm but only offerings to local customers.		The acquired firm is serving similar local customer universes as those of the other business units belonging to the corporate firm but is not addressing global and regional customers

Scenario 4: Expansion Mergers and Acquisitions The corporate firm is pursuing extending the scope of business by adding related competencies opening new market opportunities.

The acquired firm has a different strategy and is serving different customer universes than those of other business units belonging to the corporate firm.		The acquired firm has additional but related competencies and offerings compared those of the other business units belonging to the corporate firm.		The acquired firm is serving different but related customer universes compared to those of the other business units belonging to the corporate firm.

Figure 12.4 Different merger and acquisition scenarios.

- *Financial mergers and acquisitions* are related to corporate conglomerates, i.e. corporations that consist of often seemingly unrelated business units. The merger and acquisition is driven by risk and investment logics and no integration of business units is planned. Synergies are thereby only realized at a corporate level and only in financial terms.

- *Penetration mergers and acquisitions* are about adding market share by integrating a firm serving the same customer universes through similar promises and delivery patterns. The acquiring firm simply increases market share and its market penetration. These mergers and acquisitions are all about scale: "More of the same."

- *Internationalization mergers and acquisitions* are about extending the global reach of the acquiring firm. Acquiring firms merge or acquire a unit which has similar production capabilities but is located in a different region. Typically, these mergers and acquisitions are driven by the acquiring firm's customers' internationalization processes which force suppliers to follow their customers and serve them in a global setting. The alternative to a merger or acquisition is a green field investment to build production capacity. While this is a valid option, it is often inferior because the global customers do not take up enough capacity to fully support the new unit. As such, the acquiring firm is not only interested in production capacity, but also in sales volume to local customers.

- *Expansion mergers and acquisitions* are about extending the strategic scope of the acquiring firm by merging or acquiring a firm which holds competencies new to the acquiring firm. These acquired competences can be new generations of goods and services, which can be seen as an outsourcing of innovation management and subsequent, upon innovation success, insourcing of the results. Alternatively, expansion may add new customer types, or enable new roles and scenes to be addressed. Thus, the acquiring firm expands into new competitive arenas.

Financial mergers and acquisitions

In this scenario, there is only financial reasoning for the merger or acquisition. This is often related to risk and cash flow management. The aim of the merger or acquisition is not to integrate business units. As such, the situation before the merger or acquisition is not relevant. Financial mergers and acquisitions are the typical playing field for investments and capital funds which enter into the investments either to spread risk or to streamline the firm and sell it off with profit.

When making the investment to spread risk, the different businesses are kept independent from each other. In order to achieve risk optimization, the customer universes must be significantly different from each other in order to ensure that the different businesses do not follow similar business cycles. These differences imply that customer types, roles and scenes are rather different between the different units, and that synergies are only being exercised at a corporate level.

Penetration mergers and acquisitions

In a nutshell, this type of merger and acquisition just shifts market share by combining former competitors into one unit. The new firm integrates the customer base of the acquired firm into the customer portfolio of the acquiring firm. In these cases, CUBEical Thinking provides a strong platform for making the transfer and integration of customers efficient and smooth. The customers of the acquired firm are already known in terms of types, roles and scenes – they are only new in terms of being served by a "new" firm.

Assuming that the acquiring firm has already optimized its customer strategies and fulfillment procedures and aligned its different business units, significant profitable revenue growth can be generated more or less instantly when commencing the integration process. By training the customer-facing employees in the business processes applied by the other business units within the acquiring corporation and by segmenting the customers of the acquired firm along the customer types already used in the acquiring firm, the insights into the customer universes of its new customers immediately lift the customer experience and customer satisfaction. The customers in the acquired portfolio thus experience a warm, friendly and competent welcome. These types of mergers and acquisitions typically deliver immediate positive EBITDA results as the deep customer insight of the acquiring aligned firm, thus, can be easily leveraged upon by the customer-facing employees of the acquired firm. If not aligned, the acquiring firm is typically only able to realize synergies up to the level its current alignment allows for.

Internationalization mergers and acquisitions

Internationalization mergers and acquisitions typically focus on extending the global reach of the acquiring firm by integrating an acquired firm which can provide a local platform for serving the acquiring firm's global and regional customers. The globalization trend requires firms to follow their customers as they internationalize their businesses. Instead of starting their own facilities from scratch, acquiring firms often offer immediate production capacity, human resources and local customer bases.

Internationalization mergers and acquisitions pose a number of challenges. The first challenge is represented by post-merger initiatives interfering with local operations. Naturally, the acquired business unit does not operate with the corporate business processes and is thus not aligned. Alignment initiatives are aimed at realizing synergies and gaining control by imposing new reporting structures, by performing lean projects to improve production efficiency and by leveraging on the acquired firm's customer portfolios to increase up- and cross-sales. These initiatives often cause more frustration than cooperation between the acquiring and the acquired firm as there is no common understanding of who the customers are and how they should be served. Consequently, such initiatives can pose a major impact on the acquired business unit's behavior vis-à-vis its customers as change to business processes in turn changes the nature of customer relationships. Often, the resource efficiency of the acquired business unit might increase in this process but at the expense of a major setback in market efficiency.

When entering into internationalization mergers or acquisitions, executives must keep in mind that the scope of the acquired firm typically differs significantly from that of the acquiring firm. Handling this situation poses another challenge – namely to secure that the acquired firm is supported and motivated in changing its local scope towards a global and regional one. In facilitating this transition, capacity utilization of the firm's global and regional customers is typically not high enough in the beginning to support sole focus on global and regional customers. As such, the acquiring firm has to continue local business in order to run the new unit profitably. This is normally a temporary issue as the global and regional customers increase their business over time. However, in the midst of the integration process it poses a challenge for the firm to maintain business in one universe and manage global and regional business in another universe – while both universes compete internally for resources.

Therefore, local customers must be segmented according to their customer types at the time of the merger or acquisition and only thereafter can the gradual process of targeting local customers, showing above average profitability, commence in parallel with the local unit's relationships with regional and global customers gaining momentum.

To facilitate the gradual shift in focus for the acquired local unit and, thus, to extend the reach of the acquiring firm vis-à-vis its global and regional customers, the challenge is to secure that the global and regional business processes are anchored locally at the same time as the local business processes fully support the business unit in serving its local customers. From our experience in dealing with this question and appreciating the fact that local business units depend on the presence of its truly local customers, the before-mentioned concept of minimum global and regional requirements has proven to be an efficient way of allowing adaptation to local markets.

Consequently, based on the knowledge of the customer universes of the global and regional customers of the acquiring firm, knowledge can be shared and the acquired local business unit can be coached and supported in developing business with local units of these global and regional customers not yet being served locally. In doing so, the local business unit is equipped with an agenda of relevance to the firm's global and regional customers in question. Often the acquired firm can efficiently open the door to local branches of global and regional customers by presenting these with knowledge about their organizations beyond their knowledge at hand. Thus, an efficient knowledge sharing across the firm offers significant additional business value to the regional and global customer by facilitating knowledge sharing across the customer's own organization.

In this context, global and regional key account teams facilitate the local business development in selecting the specific up-and cross-sales opportunities to pursue. By supplying them with insights into the success stories from dealing with other parts of the customer's global and regional organization local interaction with customers becomes targeted and relevant.

Apart from the initiatives aimed at obtaining market reach through utilizing the acquired firm as an additional contact point to global and regional customers, CUBEical Thinking also ensures profitable revenue growth for the local customer business. Thus, local customers are being segmented and served according to their customer types and, therewith, they gradually aligned with the customer portfolios of other local business units.

As outlined in the above, in the case of integrating local business units in connection with internationalization mergers and acquisitions, CUBEical Thinking strongly supports firms in harvesting the up- and cross-sales potentials of global and regional customers by leveraging on the acquiring organization's knowledge about its best customer relationships. Furthermore, CUBEical Thinking facilitates the shift in reach and scope of the acquired local business unit.

Expansion mergers and acquisitions

In this scenario, acquiring firms add new competencies to their organization through mergers and acquisitions which enlarge the scope of their business. Competencies are understood as enablers for the acquiring firm to address new customer types or enablers for penetrating and strengthening its expansion into new business areas by addressing existing customer types in new roles and/or scenes by offering new products and services.

Expansion mergers and acquisitions are generally complex as they typically change the strategic scope not only of the acquired firm but also of the other business units within the acquiring corporation. Thus, the most demanding version of expansion mergers and acquisitions is when the enlargement is changing the overall strategy involving changes to customer types, competitive arenas being served and to goods and services offered. In that case, customer and product profitability can significantly change. Consequently, customer and product profitability have to be recalculated to guide the transition of the firm's strategic scope.

Thus, even though expansion mergers and acquisitions represent an evolution in strategy by building on extending the existing customer and product portfolio and not a radical shift in strategy, the process is very demanding and requires significant corporate guidance. Therefore, high alignment is necessary to enable a rapid change process. Also, low alignment before the merger and acquisition means little chance of actually changing the organization as the likelihood of coexisting units without integration is much higher than realizing the envisioned synergies.

In our experience, corporate guidance from headquarters in rationalizing and targeting customer and product portfolios at local, regional and global levels with the acquired competencies must be founded on a good segmentation practice linking customers and products together through the concept of the customer universes. Lacking an overview of customer differences and appropriate product portfolios leaves a firm with no chance for systematic profitable revenue growth.

Summing up mergers and acquisitions

Successful mergers and acquisitions require that the acquiring firm has aligned its operations up front. If not, a pure financial merger or acquisition will materialize where no synergies are harvested. These days, where many firms are pursuing growth through mergers and acquisitions, we too frequently meet corporations which are not aligned and for whom driving profit out of their investments seems an uphill battle with random success, if any.

The first important step in a merger or acquisition is the identification of the scenario (Figure 12.4) as this defines the fit and opportunities for success. Often difficulties arise because managers have misinterpreted the scenario and consequently manage into a suboptimal direction. CUBEical Thinking provides a framework for aligning the operations of firms and for guiding the integration process in relation to mergers and acquisitions.

Referring to Figure 12.3, without a good segmentation framework, streamlining and driving business value out of mergers and acquisitions becomes the result of gambling rather than of a neatly planned implementation of a firm's growth strategy. A growth strategy must carefully evaluate the business opportunities and turn these into a strategy map pointing out how resources should be allocated to business units, customer types and to the development of goods and services. The different merger and acquisition scenarios also result in different organizational alignments (Figure 12.5).

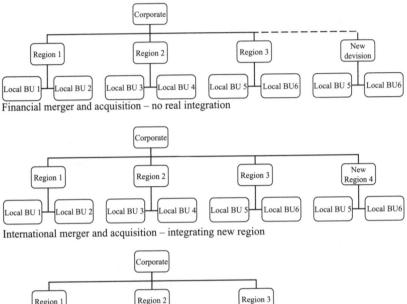

Financial merger and acquisition – no real integration

International merger and acquisition – integrating new region

Penetration/Expansion merger and acquisition – integrating new customers and/or products

Figure 12.5 Different organizational alignments of mergers and acquisitions.

Business is not about growth – it is about profitable revenue growth! It does not matter if growth is pursued through organic growth or through mergers and acquisitions; good customer segmentation is the only way to put customers at the top of the executive agenda, making customers the pivotal focus for driving profitable revenue growth.

Epilog

Gordias, a poor peasant who accidentally became king of the Phrygians when he happened to be the next man to enter the city in a wagon, dedicated the ox-cart to the Gods in gratitude. He tied it to a post with an intricate knot – and an oracle prophesied that the one to untie the knot would become king of Asia. Many tried to untie the knot but did not succeed. In 333 BC, Alexander the Great untied the knot by slicing it with his sword after having failed to find the end of the knot. Thereafter, Alexander the Great conquered Asia.

(adaped from Wikipedia)

Many managers describe their markets as a Gordian knot: there are no ends to the rope, customers and segments are intertwined. But conquering markets and winning market share are related to untying the knot. The development of a market strategy becomes an intractable problem which many have failed to solve in the past.

As Alexander demonstrated, a bold stroke is sometimes needed to solve an unsolvable problem. All he used was readily available resources and a fresh approach. Similarly, this book offers a solution to the Gordian knot of market strategy by introducing fresh thinking. The good news is that no new resources are needed and that the new thinking is easily adapted.

The basic message of this book is simple. Without customers, there is no business. And customers live in their own universe – the customer universe. The only way of successfully doing business is to understand, strategize and activate within the customer universe. Any other way will not meet the target – the customer.

While this logic is not new, our CUBEical tools for implementing are. Over the years, we have pushed the Customer Universe Based Execution towards a CUBEical Thinking framework which covers customer segmentation and, thus, market insight; market strategy and, thus, resource allocation; and day-to-day operations in marketing and sales, product development and distribution. As such, CUBEical Thinking cuts across departments and hierarchical levels – it is a way to understand business.

From our work with firms we know that executives and managers experience the impact of our method on their business strategy, their market effectiveness, and their profits as a bold stroke. So CUBEical Thinking has proven itself as an Alexandrian solution to driving profitable revenue growth inside the customer universe.

The motivation for this book came from our frustration about the low level of segmentation practice and effectiveness in firms. So there was, and still is, a good potential for improvement. We thus ventured into developing our ideas into concepts, and the results are presented in this book.

Our hope is that you enjoyed reading the book as much as we have enjoyed writing it – and that the use of our concepts has a major impact on your strategy, your marketing and sales your operations – and not to forget the top- and bottom-line of your business.

Glossary

For the development of the glossary, Wikipidia was checked for their definitions and, when found applicable, their definition was used or adapted.

Advertisement: A communication whose purpose is to inform potential customers about goods and services and how to use and obtain them. Advertisements are usually placed anywhere an audience can easily and/or frequently access visuals, audio, print etc.

Behavior: Refers to the actions or reactions of a human being or organization in relation to the firm or the employees of the firm.

Beliefs: A belief is the psychological state in which an individual holds a proposition or premise (argument) to be true without necessarily being able to adequately prove its main contention to other people who may or may not agree.

Business management framework: A consistent system of thoughts, models and tools on how to run a business successfully.

Business set-up: A firm's operation system in terms of CRM, channel, production and supply chain.

Business-to-business: Business-to-business, or "B2B", is a term commonly used to describe business transactions between businesses.

Business-to-consumer: Business-to-consumer, or "B2C", is a term commonly used to describe business transactions between a business and consumers.

Communication: Communication, here specially focused on market communication, is a process that allows organizations to exchange information with their customers by several methods such as advertising, direct mail, seminars, meetings, etc.

Competition map: Mapping of customer satisfaction as well as firm and competitors' presence across the competitive arenas of the customer and market universe map.

Corporate values: The values of a firm governing its behaviors and decision-making processes.

CUBEical: A registered trademark of Andersen&Partners Management Consulting labeling the various concepts linked to Customer Universe Based Execution.

CUBEical communication: A framework for communication based on Customer Universe Based Execution.

CUBEical implementation: A framework for realizing business objectives.

CUBEical segmentation: A segmentation framework segmenting customers along customer types, roles and scenes, fulfilling the requirements of good customer segmentation.

CUBEical selling: An approach to selling which, opposed to product selling, starts sales by explicitly addressing the needs and expectations of a customer.

CUBEical strategy: A strategy framework based on the CUBEical segmentation framework.

CUBEical Thinking: A business management framework. Consisting of three parts: CUBEical segmentation, CUBEical strategy and CUBEical implementation.

Customer expectations: Customer expectations are the views of a customer on how a firm should address the customer needs. Thus, the expectation is about the solution; the need is about the challenge to be solved. The expectation is about how the firm does a job for the customer; the need is the job itself.

Customer needs: Customer need is the outcome the customer wants to achieve; the expectation is the way this outcome is achieved. Needs are stable, expectations are dynamic and typically inflicted by the firms themselves.

Customer type: Description of customer behaviors and decision-making patterns.

Customer competition map: Mapping of customer satisfaction as well as firm and competitors' presence across the competitive arenas of a specific customer type.

Customer opportunity map: Mapping of opportunities into the customer competition map.

Customer strategy map: Mapping of strategic decisions into the customer opportunity map.

Customer universe: Mapping of the competitive arenas in which interaction with the customer type in question takes place. The universe is made up of three dimensions: customer types, roles and scenes.

Customer Universe Based Execution (CUBE): Driving business as defined in the customer strategy map.

Customer universe map: Mapping of the competitive arenas in which interaction with customers takes place.

Decisions/Decision-making: Decision-making can be regarded as an outcome of mental processes leading to the selection of a course of action among several alternatives. Every decision-making process produces a final choice. The output can be an action or an opinion.

EBITDA: Earnings Before Interest, Tax, Depreciation and Amortization. A measure to determine the strength of a business.

Firm: We use the term interchangeably with the employees of the firm. We know that firms do not interact, employees of firms do. But these employees have very different job titles, and it would make the book incomprehensive when trying to list them all. Choosing the "normal" job description may confuse readers in case a person with another job title performs a task. Thus, whenever you read firm, replace the word with the appropriate job title, or even the name of the person, or the department name.

Framework: A basic conceptual structure used to solve or address complex issues.

Map: Representation of information mapped on the three-dimensional structure made up of customer types, roles and scenes.

Market: A market is a set of social arrangements which facilitate exchange of goods and services.

Market competition map: Mapping of customer satisfaction as well as firm and competitors' presence across the competitive arenas of all customer types.

Market opportunity map: Mapping of opportunities into the market competition map.

Market strategy map: Mapping of strategic decisions into the market opportunity map.

Market universe map: Mapping of the competitive arenas in which interaction with all customer types takes place. The universe is made up of three dimensions: customer types, roles and scenes.

Mission: A brief statement of the purpose of a firm.

Opportunity: A chance for improving market performance and/or profit vis-à-vis competition.

Profitable revenue growth: Growing top-line by addressing customers providing positive, above average profits.

Revenue: Revenue or turnover is the income that the firm receives from the sale of goods and services to customers.

Roadmap: A systematic order of doing things to obtain a given result.

ROI: Return on investments.

Role: Roles are the specific relationships which a customer has vis-à-vis other people, e.g. friends and family in the private sphere or colleagues and managers in the business sphere.

Satisfaction: Evaluation of an experience with the expectations the person had before the encounter as well as against some general quality level.

Scene: Scenes are the customer touch points, where customers interact with a firm and/or its offerings. A scene is the environment in which the interaction takes place – the context of interaction.

Segmentation: Grouping of individuals or firms according common characteristics.

Set-up: See business set-up.

Strategy: Decisions on where and how to compete in order to fulfill a firm's business objectives.

Total market: The aggregation of all competitive arenas across customer types.

Type: See customer type.

Universe: The three-dimensional framework made up of the three dimensions: customer types, roles and scenes.

Values: Individuals, groups, firms, societies, or cultures have values that are largely shared by their members. The values identify those objects, conditions or characteristics that the individual and/or members consider important; that is, valuable. Value governs human behavior.

Vision: An ideal or a goal towards which a firm aspires.

Index

Compiled by Indexing Specialists (UK) Ltd